TECHNICAL AND VOCATIONAL EDUCATION AND TRAINING IN TAJIKISTAN AND OTHER COUNTRIES IN CENTRAL ASIA
KEY FINDINGS AND POLICY OPTIONS

Eiko Kanzaki Izawa, Takashi Yamano, Daler Safarov, and Jorgen Billetoft

MARCH 2021

ASIAN DEVELOPMENT BANK

 Creative Commons Attribution 3.0 IGO license (CC BY 3.0 IGO)

© 2021 Asian Development Bank
6 ADB Avenue, Mandaluyong City, 1550 Metro Manila, Philippines
Tel +63 2 8632 4444; Fax +63 2 8636 2444
www.adb.org

Some rights reserved. Published in 2021.

ISBN 978-92-9262-709-6 (print); 978-92-9262-710-2 (electronic); 978-92-9262-711-9 (ebook)
Publication Stock No. TCS210003
DOI: http://dx.doi.org/10.22617/TCS210003

The views expressed in this publication are those of the authors and do not necessarily reflect the views and policies of the Asian Development Bank (ADB) or its Board of Governors or the governments they represent.

ADB does not guarantee the accuracy of the data included in this publication and accepts no responsibility for any consequence of their use. The mention of specific companies or products of manufacturers does not imply that they are endorsed or recommended by ADB in preference to others of a similar nature that are not mentioned.

By making any designation of or reference to a particular territory or geographic area, or by using the term "country" in this document, ADB does not intend to make any judgments as to the legal or other status of any territory or area.

This work is available under the Creative Commons Attribution 3.0 IGO license (CC BY 3.0 IGO) https://creativecommons.org/licenses/by/3.0/igo/. By using the content of this publication, you agree to be bound by the terms of this license. For attribution, translations, adaptations, and permissions, please read the provisions and terms of use at https://www.adb.org/terms-use#openaccess.

This CC license does not apply to non-ADB copyright materials in this publication. If the material is attributed to another source, please contact the copyright owner or publisher of that source for permission to reproduce it. ADB cannot be held liable for any claims that arise as a result of your use of the material.

Please contact pubsmarketing@adb.org if you have questions or comments with respect to content, or if you wish to obtain copyright permission for your intended use that does not fall within these terms, or for permission to use the ADB logo.

Corrigenda to ADB publications may be found at http://www.adb.org/publications/corrigenda.

Notes:
In this publication, "$" refers to United States dollars.
ADB recognizes "Kyrgyzstan" as the Kyrgyz Republic and "Russia" as the Russian Federation.

On the cover: Participants can take various skills training programs at different vocational lyceums and centers in Tajikistan (photos by ADB).

Cover design by Claudette Rodrigo.

Contents

Tables, Figures, and Boxes	v
Acknowledgments	vii
Abbreviations	viii
Executive Summary	ix

I. Introduction — 1
    A. Independence of Central Asian Countries — 2
    B. Geographic and Demographic Features of Central Asian Countries — 3

II. Macroeconomics and Labor Market in Central Asia — 11
    A. Tajikistan — 14
    B. Other Central Asian Countries — 23

III. Technical and Vocational Education and Training History, Policies, Systems, and Performance — 35
    A. Technical and Vocational Education and Training Policies and Systems in the Former Soviet Union — 35
    B. Tajikistan — 40
    C. Other Central Asian Countries — 49

IV. ADB in Central Asia — 61
    A. Tajikistan — 61
    B. Kyrgyz Republic — 62
    C. Uzbekistan — 63

V. Many Challenges Remain — 65
    A. Technical and Vocational Education and Training Governance and Management — 65
    B. Responsiveness of Technical and Vocational Education and Training System — 66
    C. Quality and Relevance of Technical and Vocational Education and Training — 66
    D. Shortage of Jobs — 67
    E. School-to-Work Transition — 68
    F. Distance Education and E-learning — 68
    G. Regional Coordination and Collaboration — 69

VI.	**Recommendations for Future Technical and Vocational Education and Training Engagements**	**71**
	A. Increasing the Technical and Vocational Education and Training System's Responsiveness	71
	B. Quality and Efficiency of Technical and Vocational Education and Training	73
	C. Public–Private Partnerships and Industry Partnerships	75
	D. Easing School-to-Work Transition	77
	E. Gender Equality	80
	F. Information and Communication Technology and Digital Skills	80
	G. Strengthened Regional Cooperation	83
References		**85**

Tables, Figures, and Boxes

Tables

1	Population and Land Area, Selected Central Asian Countries, 2020	4
2	Population Data, Selected Central Asian Countries, 2018	4
3	Percentage of Population (both sexes combined) by Broad Age Group, 2020	6
4	Notre Dame Global Adaptation Initiative Country Index, 2018	7
5	Environmental Challenges Facing Tajikistan	7
6	Human Development Index of Central Asian Countries, 2018	8
7	Education Component of the Human Development Index, Selected Countries, 2018	9
8	Gender Inequality Index, Selected Countries, 2018	9
9	Achievement of Selected Sustainable Development Goals in Selected Commonwealth of Independent States Countries, 2018	10
10	Macroeconomic Data for Central Asian Countries, 2019	11
11	Labor Participation Rate, Selected Countries, 2018	12
12	Output per Worker, 2019	12
13	Estimates of Annual Growth Rate of Output per Worker	12
14	Value Added per Worker by Sector, 2019	13
15	Details of the United Nations E-Government Index, 2020	14
16	Human Development Index, Tajikistan, 1990–2018	16
17	Population in Multidimensional Poverty, Tajikistan, 2017	17
18	Number of Tajikistan Migrant Workers by Gender, 2015–2018	21
19	Distribution of Tajikistan Migrants Working in the Russian Federation, by Industry	22
20	Level of Education of External Labor Migrants	22
21	Technical and Vocational Education in the Soviet Union	36
22	Number of Higher Education Institutions in the Soviet Union, 1991	38
23	Profile of the Employed Population by Level of Completed Education, Labor Force Surveys, 2004, 2009, and 2016	43
24	Key Features of Education in Kazakhstan	51
25	Key Features of Education in the Kyrgyz Republic	52
26	Initial Vocational Education and Training in Turkmenistan (Vocational Schools)	54
27	Secondary Vocational Education and Training in Turkmenistan (Secondary Professional Schools)	55
28	Higher Education in Turkmenistan (Universities and Institutes)	56
29	Key Features of Education in Uzbekistan	57

30	Number of Academic Lyceums and People Enrolled in Uzbekistan	58
31	Number of Professional Colleges and People Enrolled in Uzbekistan	58
32	Number of Higher Education Institutions and People Enrolled in Uzbekistan	58

Figures

1	United Nations E-Government Index for Central Asian Countries, 2020	13
2	Value Added by Sector, Tajikistan, 2011–2018	15

Boxes

1	Competency-Based Training	47
2	Tracer Studies	72
3	Labor Market Information	72
4	Australia Skills Quality Authority	74
5	Technical and Vocational Education and Training Management Information System, South Africa	74
6	Turkey—Continuing Professional Development for Technical and Vocational Education and Training Teachers	75
7	Siemens Technical Academy, Mumbai, India	76
8	Vocational and Metallurgical College under the Tajik Aluminum Company	77
9	Singapore—Education and Career Guidance	78
10	Kazakhstan—Road Map on Employment and Socialization of Youth	79
11	Increasing Gender Responsiveness of Technical and Vocational Education and Training in Viet Nam	81
12	Online Lifelong Education Institute, Republic of Korea	82

Acknowledgments

This publication analyzes technical and vocational education and training (TVET) systems and performance in Tajikistan and other Central Asian countries and contains recommendations for policy planners and administrators. It shows the importance of TVET and the urgent need to improve it to meet labor market needs and to respond to the Sustainable Development Goals. The publication focuses primarily on the public TVET system as administered by the Ministry of Labor, Migration and Employment and Ministry of Education of Tajikistan and ministries of other countries in the region. The analysis covers labor market trends and skills sector outcomes and policy options to boost vocational skills and employability. Data collected are in tables to provide a comprehensive understanding of TVET conditions.

The study team that developed this publication was led by Eiko Kanzaki Izawa, project administration unit head of the Social Sector Division (CWSS), Central and West Asia Department (CWRD), at the Asian Development Bank (ADB). The team, which also processed the ADB-funded Skills and Employability Enhancement Project in Tajikistan, comprised Takashi Yamano, ADB senior economist; Daler Safarov, manager of the Project Administration Group of the ADB-funded Strengthening Technical and Vocational Education and Training Project / Skills and Employability Enhancement Project in Tajikistan; and Jorgen Billetoft, consultant. Rie Hiraoka, director of CWSS, reviewed the report and provided technical inputs. Madeline Dizon, project analyst, Tatiana Evstifeeva, associate external relations officer, Firuza Dodomirzoeva, senior project assistant, and Laureen Felisienne Tapnio, operations assistant, CWRD, provided coordination and administrative support.

Special thanks go to the Project Administration Group staff and consultants of the design team for the Skills and Employability Enhancement Project: Firdavs Jumaev, Khurshed Mazoriev, Ronald Cammaert, Ismat Ismatulloev, and Jamshed Kuddusov. They provided insightful and valuable inputs.

Director General	Werner Liepach, CWRD
Director	Rie Hiraoka, CWSS, CWRD
Team Leader	Eiko Kanzaki Izawa, Unit Head, Project Administration, CWSS, CWRD
Team Members	Takashi Yamano, Senior Economist, Economic Analysis and Operational Support Division, Economic Research and Regional Cooperation Department
	Daler Safarov, Manager, Project Administration Group, Strengthening Technical and Vocational Education and Training Project; and Skills and Employability Enhancement Project in Tajikistan
	Madeline S. Dizon, Project Analyst, CWSS, CWRD
	Laureen Felisienne M. Tapnio, Operations Assistant, CWSS, CWRD
	Jorgen Billetoft, Consultant

Abbreviations

ADB	Asian Development Bank
ALMP	active labor market program
CAREC	Central Asia Regional Economic Cooperation
CBT	competency-based training
CIS	Commonwealth of Independent States
COVID-19	coronavirus disease
EMIS	education management information system
EU	European Union
GDP	gross domestic product
GIZ	Deutsche Gesellschaft für Internationale Zusammenarbeit GmbH
HDI	Human Development Index
ICT	information and communication technology
ILO	International Labour Organization
IMF	International Monetary Fund
ISCO	International Standard Classification of Occupations
IVET	initial vocational education and training
LFS	Labor Force Survey
LMIS	labor market information system
NCO	National Classification of Occupations
NDS	National Development Strategy
NEET	not in employment, education, or training
OECD	Organisation for Economic Co-operation and Development
PPP	public–private partnerships
PRC	People's Republic of China
PTU	professional technical school
SOE	state-owned enterprise
SPTU	secondary professional technical school
TALCO	Tajik Aluminum Company
TVET	technical and vocational education and training
UN	United Nations
UNDP	United Nations Development Programme
VET	vocational education and training

Executive Summary

How to align technical and vocational education and training (TVET) with economic realities is high on the agenda of many governments, including those of Kazakhstan, the Kyrgyz Republic, Tajikistan, Turkmenistan, and Uzbekistan. The five Central Asian countries share their common Soviet past. While the centralized TVET model practiced in the Soviet Union was instrumental in rapidly transforming predominantly agricultural societies into economies with a strong manufacturing sector, the system lacked the flexibility to match the needs of a high-tech manufacturing and knowledge economy. Despite recent efforts by public and private agencies to modernize TVET systems, these challenges are persistent obstacles to TVET reforms.

The report's objective is to assess current TVET programs and provide recommendations for the five countries, focusing on Tajikistan, where the Asian Development Bank (ADB) has been engaged in the modernization process since 2013. Tajikistan has the youngest population and the highest population growth rate in the region. In domestic labor markets, public and state-owned enterprises (SOEs) continue to dominate industrial output although they are characterized by overemployment and low productivity. Because of the shortage of jobs at home, a substantial number of young people have opted to search for jobs abroad. In 2018, the Tajikistan government reported that almost half a million of the working-age population had left Tajikistan to look for jobs, mostly in the Russian Federation.

To clarify the situation in education and TVET, and to provide sufficient and reliable background for the study, we use information on the general situation in all the countries, focusing on Tajikistan. The background information covers the geographic and demographic situation and economic and labor market trends.

After graduating from basic education (grade 9), students in Tajikistan may enroll in general senior secondary education, secondary technical education provided by technical colleges, or initial vocational education and training (IVET) provided by vocational lyceums. IVET is provided by a network of 61 vocational lyceums under the auspices of the Ministry of Labor, Migration and Employment. The lyceums offer 1- and 2-year diploma courses to prepare students for entry into secondary and higher vocational institutions or for a job.

Senior secondary TVET is provided by 49 technical colleges managed by ministries, including the Ministry of Education and Science, and SOEs. The technical colleges offer 3- and 4-year courses to develop technicians, forepersons, and supervisors. In addition to the regular technical senior secondary programs, several technical colleges offer IVET programs and short-term training courses. Technical colleges are better equipped and enjoy better infrastructure than IVET lyceums, and secondary TVET is considered more prestigious than IVET, resulting in colleges attracting more students who pay their fees themselves. Although no tracer studies of secondary TVET graduates are available, there are indications that many graduates opt for higher education and only about 20%–25% enter the labor market upon graduation.

Reflecting the government's effort to increase the population's education achievements, more than 80% have completed secondary education and above in Tajikistan; 70% of the labor force has no formal qualification apart from a general education certificate. About 20% of new entrants to the labor market have completed higher education. In comparison, youth who completed either secondary TVET at a college or IVET accounted for 13% of the total in 2016. The percentage of the labor force with an IVET diploma has decreased, while the share of those with secondary TVET has increased. International partners, especially ADB, the European Union (EU), and Deutsche Gesellschaft für Internationale Zusammenarbeit GmbH (GIZ), have played an important role in modernizing TVET. Support includes policy advice, capacity building, development of occupational standards, updating of curricula, development and production of learning material, and training of teachers and assessors. In addition to the system-level support, the partners have financed selected equipment and material and, in the case of ADB, rehabilitation of several TVET institutions. The National Education Development Strategy 2020 assumes a transition to competency-based training in vocational education and training, modularization of programs, and adoption of a national qualification framework (NQF).

To varying degrees, the countries have launched important education reforms, including in TVET, to overcome the weaknesses inherited from the Soviet system. The common feature of the reforms is a desire to bring the education system more in line with the needs and opportunities of the economy, and to optimize utilization of available resources. Comparable to Tajikistan in its small population size and weak domestic labor market, the Kyrgyz Republic heavily relies on international remittances, which have progressively increased to the equivalent of one-third the country's gross domestic product (GDP) in recent years. There have been many attempts to reform TVET, focusing on IVET, including the shift toward learning outcomes and employer and private sector involvement.

In Kazakhstan, TVET has undergone major reforms, including the launch of a dual approach (work-based learning) and the development of professional standards. The government has established national and regional TVET councils to work with businesses and industries on plans for training personnel, forecasting the need for specialists, and developing professional standards. To involve employers, the government has given the National Chamber of Entrepreneurs the mandate to approve occupational standards and a leading role in developing occupational standards via sector associations.

The Kyrgyz Republic has developed and adopted an NQF. Some of the levels match the Russian Federation qualification system to ease recognition of qualification levels for the external labor market.

Turkmenistan remains one of the fast-growing economies in the world. The state-owned gas and oil industry accounts for more than 35% of GDP but only 14% of employment. A substantial but unknown number of young people migrate to other countries in the region. Turkey is a popular destination, followed by Kazakhstan and the Russian Federation. Secondary TVET, IVET, and higher education are provided by state and non-state education institutions. While secondary TVET and IVET are mostly paid for, higher education is mostly free. As in other Central Asian countries, TVET is provided in narrowly defined professional profiles, and in only a few cases do the students also learn general education disciplines or other subjects, leaving graduates with considerably less opportunity to continue to higher education.

In 2017, Uzbekistan launched an ambitious program of market-oriented reforms. The government has embarked on reform of TVET to ensure that it is relevant to the labor market's needs. Consequently, new TVET institutional arrangements are emerging, focusing on closer links with the labor market, the private sector, and trade unions.

Challenges and Recommendations

Shortage of jobs. Unemployment and underemployment are serious concerns for the Central Asian countries, except Kazakhstan. The situation calls for (i) efforts to further diversify the economy, which would make the countries less dependent on labor migration; and (ii) intensified use of active labor market programs such as job-placement assistance to school-leavers, wage subsidies, and start-up support to talented youth.

Quality and relevance of technical and vocational education and training. Most reform initiatives have focused on access and inclusiveness rather than quality of education. Low quality and labor market relevance of vocational education and training have several implications. First, public and private employers have difficulty recruiting people with the required qualifications. Second, TVET is less attractive among young people, who opt for the academic stream of upper secondary education and higher education instead of IVET and secondary TVET. Partnerships between public TVET institutions and private companies have proved effective in increasing resource mobilization to improve the quality of TVET.

School-to-work transition. Career counselling and guidance can ease the school-to-work transition. All the countries lack proper career guidance or orientation systems. The lack of experienced career counsellors and computer-based information programs represents a major bottleneck that prevents effective career choice for young people and adults, as well as the smooth transition from training to the labor market.

Responsiveness of technical and vocational education and training and higher education systems. None of the countries have fully developed a labor market information system (LMIS). An LMIS is useful in matching the supply of skills with employer demand and opportunities for self-employment and in guiding job seekers and students in their education choices. Information about major industries, recent growth areas, occupations experiencing shortages, and qualifications needed for jobs can help people make better-informed decisions.

Technical and vocational education and training governance and management. All the countries have undergone a transition from centralization to decentralization in governance and management of TVET and higher education. There are several ways in which TVET management can be improved: (i) establish management boards or advisory committees with external participation at each TVET institution, (ii) delegate more responsibility to the management of TVET institutions, and (iii) introduce an electronic management information system for TVET. The system will allow storage of all relevant data concerning students and their performance and teaching staff and facilities of TVET institutions.

Distance education. Supported by information and communication technology, distance education has recently started to be implemented in Central Asia and shows great potential in building lifelong systems. Indeed, e-learning can expand access to quality learning at all levels of education, including IVET and TVET. E-learning systems have a positive impact on the learning process and on the quality of teaching, paving the way for lifelong learning. The coronavirus disease (COVID-19) outbreak has accentuated the importance of developing e-learning as a supplement to conventional classroom-based learning.

Regional coordination. Considering the legacy shared by the countries and the close economic ties among them, there are considerable benefits from intensifying regional collaboration and experience sharing. In addition to TVET and higher education, labor migration is an area with obvious potential for coordination and joint initiatives.

I. Introduction

Aligning the technical and vocational education and training (TVET) system with prevailing economic realities is high on the agenda of all Central Asian governments. While most of the countries have experienced remarkable economic recovery since the collapse of the Soviet Union, growth has not led to commensurate job creation. Rather, enrollment rates for TVET have declined while general secondary schools and tertiary education have expanded. TVET reforms confront issues of quality, access, and relevance.

In this report, Central Asia is defined as Kazakhstan, the Kyrgyz Republic, Tajikistan, Turkmenistan, and Uzbekistan, five members of the former Soviet Union with common trends in major fields of development.

The report takes stock of ongoing TVET reforms in several Central Asian countries, with special attention to the school-to-work transition of new entrants to the labor market. In response to the disruptions caused by the coronavirus disease (COVID-19) pandemic, the report explores (i) distance learning for skills training using information and communication technology; (ii) the use of learning management systems; (iii) how science, technology, engineering, and mathematics education can contribute to skills development; (iv) accreditation and certification systems for skills training; (v) the use of labor market information systems to improve matching labor market needs to skills training; (vi) how to reduce the number of those not in employment, education, or training (NEET); and (vii) how to improve gender parity.

Based on an in-depth assessment of ongoing TVET reforms in Tajikistan, where ADB has been engaged in the modernization process since 2013, the report draws lines to the situation in a selection of other Central Asian countries, all former Soviet Union member states. It is the report's hypothesis that almost 30 years after the disintegration of the Soviet Union in 1991, the legacy of the Soviet education system still impacts the functioning of the countries' TVET systems and, thus, their problems.

Determining the content and variations of the Soviet legacy in education will help formulate the main problems of education and TVET and directions of reforms or developing reforms in the area. One of the main problems in education and TVET is the lack of cooperation with industries, which brings a set of problems related to the lack of school-to-work transition initiatives, labor markets not adapted to market requirements, expansion of productive employment, and others.

The Asian Development Bank (ADB) is financing several major skills programs in Central Asian countries, including the Kyrgyz Republic (Skills for Inclusive Growth Sector Development), Georgia (Modern Skills for Better Jobs Sector Development), and Uzbekistan (Skills Development for a Modern Economy. These programs are in line with ADB's technical assistance for Skills Strategies for Industrial Modernization and Inclusive Growth Project.

The objective of the research is to assess the current situation of TVET in the countries, focusing on Tajikistan, and to provide recommendations based on good practices of other countries. The recommendations will facilitate further development of TVET in the region.

The research aims to achieve the following:
(i) Review current challenges of newly independent Central Asia countries, especially Tajikistan, focusing on economic development and the labor market.
(ii) Assess the status and current situation of TVET development in the countries, especially Tajikistan, based on analyses of data and a review of reports and country research.
(iii) Identify problems in the sector, including the impact of COVID-19.
(iv) Review good practices of other countries on problematic aspects of TVET in Tajikistan and the other countries.

The analysis revolves around four points:
(i) experience from efforts to improve the quality, relevance, and efficiency of TVET;
(ii) progress of institutional reforms, including separation of delivery and regulation of TVE and employer involvement in governance;
(iii) responses to the COVID-19 crisis, including the use of online and blended learning; and
(iv) school-to-work transition initiatives.

The report draws on two sources of information: (i) for Tajikistan and Turkmenistan, a combination of observations made during two field visits and secondary sources such as government documents, research papers, available statistics, reports by national and international organizations, including the ADB-funded Tajikistan Skills and Employability Enhancement Project; and (ii) for the other Central Asia countries, secondary documentation as earlier identified. During the field visits, the team held discussions with senior government representatives and visited a wide range of TVET institutions and, in Tajikistan, private companies.

A. Independence of Central Asian Countries

During the establishment of the Soviet Union in the early 1920s the Central Asian map was redrawn according to a monoethnic principle for each major entity and its people. Each area had the formal status of a constituent autonomous socialist republic of the Soviet Union. As a full-fledged member of the Soviet Union, each republic underwent social and economic transformation. A sense of nationhood began to rise in the countries. Dams were constructed for electric power generation and irrigation and industry was developed. The Virgin and Idle Lands program launched in 1953 opened up vast grasslands for wheat farming. However, the communist political purges of the 1930s exacted heavy casualties, especially among the intelligentsia and leaders. World War II brought further cultural changes as the Soviet authorities relocated thousands of Russian, Polish, and Jewish managers, intellectuals, and cultural figures.[1] During the first 10–15 years of the Soviet era, Central Asian countries saw literacy increase dramatically and the active development of TVET systems began. TVET worked effectively during reconstruction after World War II.[2]

The Soviet Union's disintegration in 1991 led to each republic declaring independence: Kyrgyzstan and Uzbekistan on 31 August 1991, Tajikistan on 9 September 1991, Turkmenistan on 27 October 1991, and Kazakhstan on 16 December 1991. On 5 May 1993, the Republic of Kyrgyzstan changed its name to the Kyrgyz Republic. On 21 December 1991, the five Central Asian republics formally entered the new Commonwealth of Independent States (CIS).

Each new country experienced difficult situations following independence. In Tajikistan, the 1992–1997 civil war severely damaged an already weak economic infrastructure and caused a sharp decline in industrial and agricultural

---

[1] G. R. G. Hamby, D. R. Smith, E. Allworth, and D. Sinor. 2017. History of Central Asia.
[2] L. V. Zakharovsky. 2015. The Soviet System of Vocational Education and the Process of Mobilization Modernization in the Soviet Union. *Scientific Dialogue*. 5 (41).

production.³ The fighting had left tens of thousands dead and had displaced more than a half million people. In between 1993 and 1997 in Turkmenistan, the quality of life did not improve despite foreign investment in natural gas and the economy contracted. Kazakhstan faced serious economic challenges throughout the 1990s.⁴

Unlike other countries in the former Soviet Union, Uzbekistan opted to pursue gradual transformation reforms.⁵ It promoted an import-substitution strategy heavily driven by state investments, often implemented through directed credit to state-owned enterprises (SOEs); introduced foreign exchange controls; and imposed tariff and nontariff barriers on foreign trade. Public sector companies and connected businesses enjoyed preferential access to physical and financial resources while being sheltered from domestic and external competition. Some economists claimed that the "Uzbek model" limited the impact of the collapse of the Soviet Union, and the country managed to recover its pre-independence gross domestic product (GDP) level by 1999. However, continued reliance on state control, particularly in agriculture and cotton production, resulted in high levels of rural poverty and outmigration of labor (footnote 5).

The five countries are similar in economic development and demographic situation based on their common Soviet past and relations with the Russian Federation. Despite some periods of tension, relations with the Russian Federation since independence have remained close, marked by economic partnership, treaties of accord, and cooperation on matters of security and intelligence. Russian continues to function as an official language in Kazakhstan and the Kyrgyz Republic and is still is widely spoken in cities in Tajikistan, Turkmenistan, and Uzbekistan as a language of interethnic communication. Regional integration is gaining importance as bilateral and multilateral relations develop.

B. Geographic and Demographic Features of Central Asian Countries

The region covered by Kazakhstan, the Kyrgyz Republic, Tajikistan, Turkmenistan, and Uzbekistan stretches from the Caspian Sea in the west to the People's Republic of China (PRC) and Mongolia in the east, and from Afghanistan and Iran in the south to the Russian Federation in the north. Central Asia is a huge region of varied geography, including high passes and mountains, large deserts, and treeless, grassy steppes. Much of the land is too dry or too rugged for farming. Agricultural land is mostly desert and mountain pastures. Arable land suitable for crop production is less than 10% of the total land. The main sources of water are the Syr Darya and the Amu Darya, mostly fed by snows and glaciers from the Pamir, Hindu Kush, and Tian Shan mountain ranges. The major lakes include the Aral Sea, between Uzbekistan and Kazakhstan, and Lake Balkhash, in Kazakhstan, both of which have shrunk significantly in recent decades because of diversion of water from rivers for irrigation and industry. Kazakhstan and Turkmenistan border the Caspian Sea, which has no natural exit. None of the five countries have access to oceans. Water is an extremely valuable resource in arid Central Asia and can lead to significant international disputes.

The most significant crops are cotton, rice, and wheat. Only Kazakhstan does not cultivate significant amounts of cotton. Cotton production relies heavily on irrigation. More than 80% of arable land in the Kyrgyz Republic, Tajikistan, Turkmenistan, and Uzbekistan is irrigated. Kazakhstan, with its wheat-based crop production, irrigates only 7% of its arable land.⁶ The emphasis on intensive cotton cultivation played a major role in the drying and polluting of the Aral Sea because of the large amounts of water and fertilizer used in cotton cultivation. Mono-crop cultivation during the Soviet period exhausted the soil and contributed to soil erosion, which still adversely affect yields (footnote 6).

---

3 ADB. 2016. *Country Partnership Strategy: Tajikistan 2016–2020*. Manila.
4 ADB. 2017. *Country Partnership Strategy: Kazakhstan, 2017–2021—Promoting Economic Diversification, Inclusive Development, and Sustainable Growth*. Manila.
5 ADB. 2019. *Country Partnership Strategy: Uzbekistan, 2019–2023—Supporting Economic Transformation*. Manila.
6 ADB. 2012. *Regional: Preparation of Sector Road Maps for Central and West Asia (Kazakhstan)*. Manila.

Its location at the crossroads of Europe and East Asia, and of South Asia and West Asia, will shape the region's long-term challenges and opportunities (footnote 4). However, the region is landlocked and difficult terrain impinges on the countries' ability to export products. Transport is an economic driver and supply chain logistics play a critical role.

The population is unevenly distributed, concentrated in cultivated lands and industrialized urban areas. Most people live in rural areas. Although Kazakhstan has a higher level of urbanization than other Central Asian countries, only 57.5% of the population lives in urban areas (Tables 1 and 2). Tajikistan is the most rural country, with 72.9% of the population living in rural areas.

Kazakhstan. Kazakhstan is by far the largest country in the region and the ninth largest in the world, but it is sparsely populated with the lowest population density of the five countries (Table 1). Urban settlements are concentrated in the southeast near the border with Uzbekistan and the Kyrgyz Republic, with three cities (Almaty, Shymkent, and

Table 1: Population and Land Area, Selected Central Asian Countries, 2020

	KAZ	KGZ	TAJ	TKM	UZB
Population (million)	18.777	6.524	9.593	6.031	33.469
Land area (km^2)	2,669,700	191,800	139,960	469,960	425,400
Agriculture land (%)	80.4	55.0	34.1	72.0	62.9
Arable land (%)	10.9	6.7	5.3	4.1	10.3
Density (per km^2)	7	34	68	13	79
Population growth rate (%)	1.21	1.69	2.32	1.50	1.48
Median age (years)	30.7	26.0	22.4	26.9	27.8

KAZ = Kazakhstan, KGZ = Kyrgyz Republic, km^2 = square kilometer, TAJ = Tajikistan, TKM = Turkmenistan, UZB = Uzbekistan.
Source: United Nations Department of Economic and Social Affairs Population Dynamics (UN estimates 1 July 2020) (accessed 3 October 2020).

Table 2: Population Data, Selected Central Asian Countries, 2018

	KAZ	KGZ	TAJ	TKM	UZB
Population (million)	18.28	6.47	9.10	5.85	32.96
in which as %					
- Female	51.5	50.5	49.6	50.8	50.1
- Male	46.5	49.5	50.4	49.2	49.9
by location as %					
- Urban	57.5	36.6	27.1	51.6	50.4
- Rural	42.5	63.4	72.9	48.4	49.6
GDP per capita ($, 2019)	**9,731**	**1,309**	**871**	**15,196**	**7,289**
Life expectancy at birth (years)	73.2	71.4	70.9	68.1	71.6
by gender as %					
- Female	77.2	75.6	73.2	71.6	73.7
- Male	68.7	67.4	68.7	64.6	69.4
Fertility rate (births per woman)	2.8	3.3	3.6	2.8	2.4

GDP = gross domestic product, KAZ = Kazakhstan, KGZ = Kyrgyz Republic, TAJ = Tajikistan, TKM = Turkmenistan, UZB = Uzbekistan.
Source: World Bank. World Development Indicators. 2020 (accessed 3 October 2020).

Taraz) accounting for half of the urban population. The country's large area and low population have clear implications for transport costs (footnote 4). Lowlands make up one-third of Kazakhstan's huge expanse, plateaus and plains account for nearly half, and low mountainous regions for about one-fifth. Table 1 shows that Kazakhstan has the largest percentage of land available for agriculture and the largest area of arable land suitable for growing crops.

The economy remains heavily dependent on hydrocarbons and is largely driven by capital-intensive extractive industries.[7] Intensive energy use has had detrimental environmental impacts and overall economic growth is vulnerable to adverse effects of climate change (footnote 2). The high rates of economic growth before the oil price drop created externalities such as environmental pollution from industrial and household waste, a coal-based energy mix with a virtual absence of renewable sources of energy, and a generally high energy intensity because of inefficiencies and subsidies. Pollution increasingly limits the quality of life, especially in cities, with rising levels of air pollution from stationary and mobile sources and growing solid waste. The rural poor suffer the most from these effects, as their income does not allow for costly substitutes or relocation. The frequency and magnitude of extreme climatic events such as heatwaves, heavy snow, and sleet, as well as floods are expected to rise. While Kazakhstan has low vulnerability to climate change, agriculture, water resources, and transport are vulnerable to risks associated with uncertain changes in precipitation, rising aridity, and extreme weather events.[8]

Kazakhstan struggles to balance regional disparities in the quality of road, energy, social, water, and sanitation infrastructure between the few economic centers and the vast periphery because of the large territory and the Soviet legacy of single-industry cities (footnote 2).

Kyrgyz Republic. Its great distance from the oceans and the sharp change of elevation from adjacent plains strongly influence the country's climate. Deserts and plains surround the Kyrgyz Republic on the north, west, and southeast, in striking contrast with the climate and landscape of the mountainous interior. The lower parts of its fringing ranges lie in belts of high temperature and receive hot, drying winds from the deserts beyond. Predominantly mountainous, the country is subject to extreme environmental conditions and vulnerability. Major environment-related challenges impacting sustainable development include land degradation, threats to agriculture production and food security, and natural hazards.[9]

The country has a narrow economic base, dominated by production and export of gold (footnote 6). Non-gold industries have stagnated because of low competitiveness. Hydropower generation is a key growth driver, but annual electricity exports have fallen by more than half since 2007 because of water management issues and the disrepair of generation assets and transmission and distribution systems.

Tajikistan. It is the smallest of the five countries (Table 1). It has the smallest percentage of land available for agriculture production and the second-lowest amount of arable land. The rugged terrain of the Pamir, Tien-Shan, and Gissar-Alay mountains occupies 93% of the country (footnote 1). The valleys, although important for human geography, make up less than 10% of the country's area. More than a thousand mountain glaciers containing 550 cubic kilometers of freshwater cover 6% of the land mass.

The mountainous geography with glacier-fed rivers has significant implications for development. Tajikistan is ranked eighth in the world in terms of hydropower potential, with about 220 terawatt-hours technically recoverable, but most hydropower plants require rehabilitation as they were built during the Soviet era (footnote 4). However, it is

---

[7] Extractive industries amount to about 30% of GDP—almost half of budget revenues and more than two-thirds of exports. Organisation for Economic Co-operation and Development (OECD). 2016. *Multi-dimensional Review of Kazakhstan: Volume 1. Initial Assessment.* Paris.
[8] ADB. 2017. *Country Partnership Strategy: Kazakhstan, 2017–2021—Promoting Economic Diversification, Inclusive Development, and Sustainable Growth.* Manila.
[9] ADB. 2018. *Country Partnership Strategy: Kyrgyz Republic 2018–2022—Supporting Sustainable Growth, Inclusion, and Regional Cooperation.* Manila.

hoped that the Rogun Hydropower Plant being constructed on the upper reaches of the Vakhsh River will generate a large amount of electricity. The project was conceptualized in the 1950s and 1960s by the Soviet Union, with construction starting in 1980 but halted following independence.[10] Construction restarted in 2008. Power was first generated in 2018 and the dam is anticipated to be the highest and tallest in the world. Part of the project's electrical output will be sold to neighboring countries and conveyed using the Central Asia–South Asia power project (CASA-1000) transmission line. The reservoir created by the dam will irrigate 300,000 hectares of arid land and reduce sedimentation in the existing Nurek Dam.

Among the countries, Tajikistan has the youngest population (median age 22.4 years), the highest population growth rate, and the highest fertility rate (Table 2): 37.3% of the population is less than 15 years old, with young people aged 15–24 years making up 17.2% of the total population, those aged 25–49 years comprising 32.4%, with just 13.1% aged over 50 years (Table 3). With most people under the age of 25 and a population growth rate of 2.32% per year (Table 1), population projections indicate that, in the next 2 decades, the number of children, particularly those 5–14 years old, will continue to increase by as much as 10%. Such trends create a demographic setting where the young-age dependency ratio is relatively high and old-age dependency ratio low, with many young workers entering the labor force. This "youth bulge" will require government policies and actions to ensure that education and employment opportunities exist and that a "demographic dividend" does not materialize. The youth bulge will expand the demand for public services and the need for human capital investments.

Tajikistan is affected by frequent disasters such as earthquakes, flooding, landslides, and avalanches (footnote 1). Under the Global Adaptation Index vulnerability rating, it is ranked the most vulnerable to the adverse effects of climate change in Central Asia (Table 4). Climate projections up to 2100 forecast a decrease in average precipitation and an increase in droughts. Table 5 shows the environmental challenges.

Turkmenistan. Only 4.1% of its total available area is cultivable (Table 1) because of the vast expanse of the Karakum desert. Most agricultural land is pasture. The total irrigated area increased substantially from 970,000 hectares at independence in 1991.[11] Under the Global Adaptation Index vulnerability rating, Turkmenistan is ranked second-most vulnerable to the adverse effects of climate change in Central Asia but is the least ready to adapt to changes and has the lowest overall Notre Dame Global Adaptation Initiative score (Table 4). Water resources and agriculture are two critical areas that are vulnerable to climate change and whose sustainability is at risk. Agriculture experiences recurrent emergency situations caused by high winds, landslides, earthquakes, and droughts, which hurt livelihoods and infrastructure. Since country derives more than 90% of its total renewable surface water resources from other countries and is vulnerable not only to local factors of climate change but also

Table 3: Percentage of Population (both sexes combined) by Broad Age Group, 2020

Country	0–14	15–24	25–49	50+
Kazakhstan	29.1	11.8	36.0	23.1
Kyrgyz Republic	32.6	15.5	34.8	17.0
Tajikistan	37.3	17.2	32.4	13.1
Turkmenistan	30.8	15.7	36.5	17.0
Uzbekistan	28.8	15.9	37.9	17.4

Source: United Nations Department of Economic and Social Affairs Population Dynamics (UN estimates as of 1 July 2020) (accessed 3 October 2020).

---

[10] Power Technology. Undated. Rogun Hydropower Plant (accessed 8 October 2020).
[11] ADB. 2017. *Country Partnership Strategy: Turkmenistan, 2017–2021—Catalyzing Regional Cooperation and Integration, and Economic Diversification.* Manila.

Table 4: Notre Dame Global Adaptation Initiative Country Index, 2018

Country	ND-GAIN High Scores Better	Vulnerability Low Scores Better	Readiness High Scores Better
Kazakhstan	56.7	0.353	0.487
Kyrgyz Republic	49.9	0.373	0.372
Tajikistan	43.8	0.535	0.305
Turkmenistan	41.7	0.406	0.239
Uzbekistan	47.6	0.403	0.354

ND-GAIN = Notre Dame Global Adaptation Initiative.
Note: The ND-GAIN Country Index summarizes a country's vulnerability to climate change and other global challenges in combination with the country's readiness to improve resilience. Vulnerability measures a country's exposure, sensitivity, and ability to adapt to the negative impact of climate change. Readiness measures a country's ability to leverage investments and convert them to adaptation actions.
Source: University of Notre Dame Global Adaptation Initiative (accessed 8 October 2020).

Table 5: Environmental Challenges Facing Tajikistan

Environmental Aspect	Issues
Water	Inadequate management of water resources causing national and transboundary problems related to water quantity and quality, contamination of ground and surface water for drinking and irrigation, poor access of the rural population to drinking water
Land	Salinization, exhaustion, and degradation of irrigated lands; water and wind erosion; pastureland degradation (85% of pasture area is reported to be degraded)
Waste	Poor management of hazardous and toxic industrial waste; unauthorized dumpsites and waste burning
Natural hazards	Prone to high-impact disasters such as floods, mudflows, landslides, and earthquakes
Energy	Environmental consequences of the winter energy deficit and the poor use of renewable energy sources other than hydroelectric energy
Biodiversity	Anthropogenic pressure on wildlife habitats and biodiversity

Sources: ADB. 2016. *Environment Assessment (Summary)* appendix to *Country Partnership Strategy: Tajikistan, 2016–2020*. Manila.

to basin-wide factors. Annual average temperatures may rise by up to 3°C by mid-century. River flow and water availability are expected to decline because of increased evapotranspiration under higher temperatures, declining precipitation, and retreating glacial sources upstream. Climate change is expected to worsen existing water stresses resulting from a growing population and economy and negatively impact agricultural output and yield. Rising average temperatures and extreme temperature events might damage infrastructure and jeopardize human health.

Uzbekistan. Of the five countries, Uzbekistan has the largest population and highest population density (Table 1). The population and economic centers are in the Fergana Valley (Andijan, Fergana, and Namangan) and the central part of the country (including Samarkand and Tashkent). However, these subnational units are not well connected by the transport system. The most direct route between them is through Tajikistan (footnote 4).

Uzbekistan has considerable mineral resources, particularly fossil fuels. About 22% of gas production is exported, generating significant revenues (footnote 3). The country possesses sizeable uranium reserves and important solar and wind renewable resources.

Water scarcity is one of the main threats constraining development (footnote 3). The country faces many problems related to shortage, pollution, and overextraction of available water sources. The quality of water resources remains unsatisfactory because of the large-scale use of chemicals for cotton cultivation, inefficient irrigation, and poor drainage systems. The low operating efficiency of wastewater treatment plants contributes to increasing the concentration of pollutants in surface water streams and depression reservoirs. The degradation of water resources results in increased morbidity rates (kidney, oncological, and acute infectious diseases) and adult and child mortality rates. About 82% of total water consumption is provided for by the transboundary water resources of the Amu Darya and the Syr Darya. Tajikistan and Uzbekistan have discussed the possible impact of the Rogun hydropower project on Uzbekistan's cotton irrigation systems.

Water–energy linkages date back to Soviet-era strategic agreements, with no cost considerations (footnote 3). The Kyrgyz Republic and Tajikistan released water in summer for cotton and food crop irrigation in Kazakhstan and Uzbekistan. As part of the deal, the former received gas and oil during winter and traded electricity with the latter. After independence, agreements for this water–energy exchange have become significantly harder to establish.

A vast irrigation network and a crop structure were established during the Soviet era (footnote 4). In 1960, the rapid increase of irrigation needs, especially for cotton cultivation, triggered the area reduction of the Aral Sea. By 2007, it covered only 10% of its original surface.[12] Losses of water in agriculture are huge because of the degraded irrigation infrastructure and the application of obsolete irrigation techniques. Water resources are, to an increasing degree, the key limitation on food production.

Human development. The United Nations (UN) Human Development Index (HDI) is a summary measure for assessing long-term progress in three basic dimensions of human development: a long and healthy life, access to knowledge, and a decent standard of living. Of the five countries, Kazakhstan has the highest HDI and is ranked 50th out of 188 countries (Table 6). Tajikistan's HDI of 0.656 is the lowest among the Central Asian countries but above the average of 0.634 for countries in the medium human development group and below the average of 0.779 for countries in Europe and Central Asia. In comparison, the Kyrgyz Republic and Uzbekistan, which are close to Tajikistan and whose population sizes are similar to Tajikistan's, ranked 122 and 108, respectively.

The HDI's education component provides an overview of the education system in Tajikistan relative to its neighbors (Table 7). In Tajikistan, both the expected years of schooling and mean years of schooling for males are higher than for females. The overall educational index for Tajikistan is lower than the other countries, except for Turkmenistan, because almost all the elements of the index are lower than the other countries, indicating that, overall, the education system is not performing as well as its neighbors'. Unfortunately, these indicators are about inputs to the system as Tajikistan does not have any system to measure student performance relative to international

Table 6: Human Development Index of Central Asian Countries, 2018

	KAZ	KGZ	TAJ	TKM	UZB
Human development index (HDI)	0.817	0.674	0.656	0.710	0.710
Life expectancy at birth	73.2	71.3	70.9	68.1	71.6
Expected years of schooling	15.3	13.4	11.4	10.9	12.0
Mean years of schooling	11.8	10.9	10.7	9.8	11.5
GNI per capita (2011 PPP, $)	22,168	3,317	3,482	16,407	6,462
HDI rank	50	122	125	108	108

GNI = gross national income, KAZ = Kazakhstan, KGZ = Kyrgyz Republic, PPP = purchasing power parity, TAJ = Tajikistan, TKM = Turkmenistan, UZB = Uzbekistan.
Source: United Nations Development Programme. 2019. *Human Development Report.*

---

[12] By 2020, efforts to reverse the decline of the Aral Sea had resulted in an increase to 15% of the original surface.

Table 7: Education Component of the Human Development Index, Selected Countries, 2018

	KAZ	KGZ	TAJ	TKM	UZB
Education index	0.817	0.734	0.673	0.628	0.718
Expected years of schooling	15.3	13.4	11.4	10.9	12.0
Expected years of schooling, females	15.6	13.6	10.9	10.5	11.8
Expected years of schooling, males	14.9	13.2	12.3	11.1	12.2
Government expenditure on education (% of gross domestic product)	2.9	7.2	5.2	NA	6.4
Gross enrollment ratio (GER), primary (% of primary school-age population)	105	108	99	88	103
GER, secondary (% of secondary school-age population)	113	98	87	86	93
GER, tertiary (% of tertiary school-age population)	53	44	31	8	9
Mean years of schooling	11.8	10.9	10.7	9.8	11.5
Mean years of schooling, females	11.9	11.0	10.1	NA	11.3
Mean years of schooling, males	11.7	10.8	11.2	NA	11.8

KAZ = Kazakhstan, KGZ = Kyrgyz Republic, NA = not available, TAJ = Tajikistan, TKM = Turkmenistan, UZB = Uzbekistan.
Source: CEIC. Tajikistan Education Statistics; and United Nations Development Programme. 2019. *Human Development Report.*

performance standards. However, the most recent Organisation for Economic Co-operation and Development (OECD) Program for International Student Assessment (PISA) results in Kazakhstan indicate cause for concern.[13]

Gender parity. The Gender Inequality Index of the United Nations Development Programme (UNDP) measures gender inequality in three aspects of human development—reproductive health, empowerment, and economic status (Table 8). Of the five countries, Kazakhstan has the lowest inequality index. Tajikistan has the

Table 8: Gender Inequality Index, Selected Countries, 2018

	KAZ	KGZ	TAJ	TKM	UZB
Gender Inequality Index	0.203	0.381	0.377	NA	0.303
Reproductive health					
Adolescent birth rate (births per 1,000 women aged 15–19)	29.8	32.8	57.1	24.4	23.8
Maternal mortality ratio (deaths per 100,000 live births)	12	60	32	42	36
Empowerment					
Share of seats in parliament (% held by women)	22.1	19.2	20.0	24.8	16.4
Population with at least some secondary education, female (% aged 25 and older)	98.3	98.6	98.8	NA	99.9
Economic status					
Labor market participation rate (% aged 15 and older), female	65.3	48.0	27.8	52.8	53.4
Labor market participation rate (% aged 15 and older), male	77.1	75.8	59.7	78.2	78.0

KAZ = Kazakhstan, KGZ = Kyrgyz Republic, NA = not available, TAJ = Tajikistan, TKM = Turkmenistan, UZB = Uzbekistan.
Source: United Nations Development Programme. 2019. Human Development Report.

---

[13] OECD. 2019. *PISA 2018 Results (Volume I): What Students Know and Can Do.* Geneva. Kazakhstan students were below the OECD average in reading (387 vs. the average of 487), mathematics (423 vs. the average of 489), and science (397 vs. the average of 489). Only 36% performed at the minimum level in reading.

Table 9: Achievement of Selected Sustainable Development Goals in Selected Commonwealth of Independent States Countries, 2018

	Sustainable Development Goals	KAZ	KGZ	TAJ	TKM	UZB
1.1.1	Population living below national poverty line (%)	4.2	22.4	27.4	NA	11.4
2.1.1	Prevalence of undernourishment (%)	<2.5	7.1	NA	5.5	7.4
2.2.1	Prevalence of stunting among children below 5 (%)	8.0	11.8	17.5	11.5	NA
3.1.1	Maternal mortality ratio (per 100,000 live births)	12	60	32	42	36
3.2.1	Under-5 mortality ratio (per 100,000 live births)	10	19	34	47	23
3.3.2	Tuberculosis incidence (per 100,000 population)	66	116	85	43	73
4.2.2	Participation rate in organized learning (1 year before official primary age) (%)	63.9	91.3	12.5	NA	36.9
5.5.1	Proportion of seats held by women in national parliament (%)	22.1	19.2	20.0	24.8	16.4
6.1.1	Proportion of population using safe drinking water (%)	NA	68.2	47.4	86.1	51.2
7.2.1	Renewable energy as share of energy (%)	2.0	24.5	43.9	0.1	3.2
8.2.1	Annual growth rate of real GDP per employed person (%)	3.3	2.9	3.8	4.7	4.6
8.5.2	Unemployment rate (%)	4.9	6.3	10.9	3.8	5.2
8.5.2	Unemployment rate (%), female	5.6	7.5	9.7	2.1	5.0
8.5.2	Unemployment rate (%), male	4.2	5.6	11.5	5.0	5.4
8.10.2	Proportion of population with bank account (%)	58.7	39.9	47.0	40.6	37.1
12.2.2	Domestic material consumption (million metric tons per capita)	29.1	8.4	3.5	16.5	9.1
17.3.2	Volume of remittances in $ as proportion of GDP (%)	0.2	33.2	31.3	0.0	3.7

GDP = gross domestic product, KAZ = Kazakhstan, KGZ = Kyrgyz Republic, NA = not available, TAJ = Tajikistan, TKM = Turkmenistan, UZB = Uzbekistan.
Source: ADB. Statistical and Data Innovation Unit 2020. *Basic 2020 Statistics*. Manila.

highest adolescent birth rate, reflecting that females tend to marry young. The shares of seats in parliament across the five countries and other CIS countries are similar but lower than in many other countries.[14] Although the education system has achieved near gender parity in enrollment for general secondary levels, Table 8 shows that in Tajikistan, Turkmenistan, and Uzbekistan, males can expect to receive more years of schooling, and in Tajikistan and Uzbekistan, the mean years of schooling are higher for males. There is evidence that gender stereotyping persists in the choice of vocational training and university degrees (footnote 6).

Sustainable Development Goals. The 17 Sustainable Development Goals (SDGs) were adopted by all UN Member States in 2015 to end poverty, protect the planet, and improve the lives and prospects of everyone, everywhere. ADB Basic Statistics reports provide an overview of the achievement of the SDGs in selected CIS countries (Table 9). For most parameters, Tajikistan lags significantly behind its neighbors, especially Kazakhstan, but also Turkmenistan and Uzbekistan. Tajikistan is far ahead of other countries only in renewable energy because of its development of hydropower.

---

[14] The Russian Federation has 16.1%, Argentina 39.5%, Cuba 53.2%, Finland 42.0%, Rwanda 55.7%, and South Africa 41.8%.

II. Macroeconomics and Labor Market in Central Asia

The five economies have transitioned from Soviet-era centrally planned economies to some version of a market economy, although vestiges of the Soviet system are still evident. Kazakhstan has the largest economy, with the largest GDP and the highest GDP per capita, while Tajikistan has the lowest GDP and lowest GDP per capita (Table 10). Before the outbreak of COVID-19, all the economies were projected to have robust GDP growth. The service sector contributes the most to GDP in Kazakhstan, the Kyrgyz Republic, and Tajikistan; the sector is a close second to industry and construction in Uzbekistan. Agriculture contributes more to GDP in Tajikistan than in the other three countries.

Tajikistan has the lowest employment–population ratio and the lowest percentage of labor force participation (Table 11). The country has the lowest rate of female participation in the labor force and the highest percentage of employment in agriculture, but only 19.2% of its GDP comes from the sector (Table 11). Uzbekistan has 33.4% of employment in agriculture, with 25.5% of GDP from the sector.

Kazakhstan has the highest level of productivity (Table 12), which is slightly higher than the Russian Federation's at $52,971.[15] The Kyrgyz Republic is the least productive and its productivity growth is projected to be low. Tajikistan has the next-lowest level of productivity and a low projected increase in productivity (Table 13). Before the

Table 10: Macroeconomic Data for Central Asian Countries, 2019

	KAZ	KGZ	TAJ	TKM	UZB
GDP ($ billion, current)	180.2	8.5	8.1	40.8	57.9
GDP per capita ($, current)	9,371.1	1,309.4	870.8	6,966.6	1,724.8
GNI per capita ($, atlas method)	8,810.0	1,240.0	1,030.0	6,740.0	1,800.0
GDP annual growth (% in constant $)	4.5	4.5	7.0	6.2	5.6
Agriculture, forestry, and fishing	0.9	2.6	4.0	NA	2.5
Industry, including construction	6.3	8.4	10.4	NA	10.6
and Services	3.9	3.3	7.0	NA	5.2
Percentage of GDP					
Agriculture, forestry, and fishing	4.4	12.1	19.2	NA	25.5
Industry, including construction	33.1	8.4	27.4	NA	33.2
services	55.5	50.2	42.1	NA	32.2

GDP = gross domestic product, GNI = gross national income, KAZ = Kazakhstan, KGZ = Kyrgyz Republic, NA = not applicable, TAJ = Tajikistan, TKM = Turkmenistan, UZB = Uzbekistan.
Source: World Bank. World Development Indicators (accessed 28 October 2020).

---

[15] By comparison, Luxembourg has the highest labor productivity in the world at $199,367 per worker. Ireland's is at $155,654 and the United States' $116,384.

Table 11: Labor Participation Rate, Selected Countries, 2018

	KAZ	KGZ	TAJ	TKM	UZB
Employment–population ratio (% aged 15 and older)	67.3	57.2	38.9	62.7	62.1
Employment in agriculture (% of total employment)	15.0	26.5	51.1	22.8	33.4
Employment in services (% of total employment)	63.7	51.3	32.2	43.5	36.3
Labor force participation rate (% aged 15 and older)	70.8	61.6	43.6	65.1	65.5
Labor force participation rate (% aged 15 and older), female	65.2	48.0	27.8	52.8	53.4
Labor force participation rate (% aged 15 and older), male	77.1	75.8	59.7	78.2	78

KAZ = Kazakhstan, KGZ = Kyrgyz Republic, TAJ = Tajikistan, TKM = Turkmenistan, UZB = Uzbekistan.
Source: United Nations Development Programme. 2020. *Human Development Report*.

Table 12: Output per Worker, 2019

(gross domestic product, constant 2011 international $ in purchasing power parity)

Country	
Kazakhstan	54,378
Kyrgyz Republic	9,293
Tajikistan	13,345
Turkmenistan	41,835
Uzbekistan	14,883

Source: International Labour Organization. Labour Productivity (accessed 19 October 2020).

Table 13: Estimates of Annual Growth Rate of Output per Worker

(gross domestic product, constant 2011 international $ in purchasing power parity) (%)

Country	2012	2016	2020	2024
Kazakhstan	3.7	1.6	3.8	3.7
Kyrgyz Republic	-0.1	3.8	2.6	2.7
Tajikistan	5.4	5.3	2.4	2.3
Turkmenistan	8.9	4.8	5.0	5.0
Uzbekistan	5.7	4.1	4.8	5.0

Note: Projections were made before the outbreak of COVID 19.
Source: International Labour Organization. Labour Productivity (accessed 19 October 2020).

Table 14: Value Added per Worker by Sector, 2019
(constant 2010 $)

Country	Agriculture, Forestry, and Fishing	Industry (including construction)	Services
Kazakhstan	6,790	45,248	21,183
Kyrgyz Republic	2,001	3,947	2,612
Tajikistan	1,819	9,296	4,702
Uzbekistan	5,737	4,989	4,713

Source: World Bank. World Development Indicators (accessed 22 October 2020).

COVID-19 pandemic impacted the world economy, the International Labour Organization (ILO) was projecting that world productivity would increase by 2.5% in 2020, Europe and Central Asia productivity by 1.9%, and lower-middle-income countries' productivity by 4.1%. The estimated growth in productivity for 2020 and 2024 for all five countries compares favorably with these averages. Looking at value added per worker by sector (Table 14), industry has the highest level of productivity and agriculture the least. The productivity of agriculture in Tajikistan is particularly low.

The effective use of computers is a means of improving productivity. The UN E-Government Development Index (Figure 1) assesses website development patterns in a country, incorporating access characteristics such as infrastructure and education levels, to reflect how a country is using information technology to promote access and inclusion. The index is a composite measure of three important dimensions of e-government: provision of online services, telecommunication connectivity, and human capacity. In Kazakhstan, there seems to be a relationship between productivity and the index, which is the highest among the countries (Table 15). Tajikistan rates low in productivity and on the index. However, Turkmenistan has the lowest index but the second-highest output per worker.

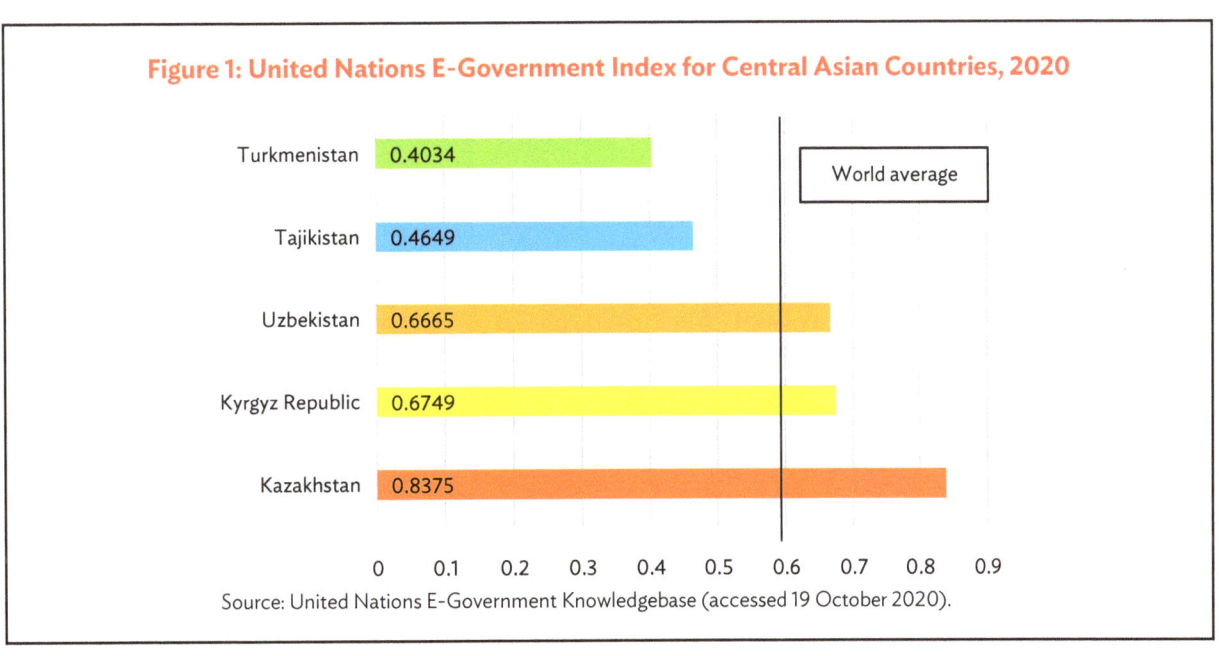

Figure 1: United Nations E-Government Index for Central Asian Countries, 2020

Source: United Nations E-Government Knowledgebase (accessed 19 October 2020).

Table 15: Details of the United Nations E-Government Index, 2020

Country	E-Govt Rank	E-Govt Index	E-Participation Index	Online Service Index	Human Capital Index	Telecommunication Infrastructure Index
Kazakhstan	29	0.8375	0.8810	0.9235	0.8866	0.7024
Kyrgyz Republic	83	0.6749	0.7143	0.6471	0.7873	0.5902
Tajikistan	133	0.4649	0.3452	0.3176	0.7274	0.3496
Turkmenistan	158	0.4034	0.2024	0.1765	0.6783	0.3555
Uzbekistan	87	0.6665	0.8095	0.7824	0.7434	0.4736

govt = government.
Source: United Nations E-Government Knowledgebase (accessed 19 October 2020).

A. Tajikistan

Macroeconomic Overview

The 1992–1997 civil war that followed immediately after Tajikistan's independence from the former Soviet Union severely damaged already weak economic infrastructure and caused a sharp decline in industrial and agricultural production. However, over the past decades, Tajikistan has made steady progress in reducing poverty and growing its economy. In 2000–2018, the poverty rate fell from 83.0% of the population to 27.4%, while the economy grew at an average rate of 7.0% per year.[16] Despite the growing economy, Tajikistan remains among the poorest of the former Soviet Union in terms of GDP per capita (Table 2). Tajikistan ranks 148th in terms of GDP per capita,[17] and 125th out of 189 countries in terms of the HDI (Table 6).

Tajikistan is a small, landlocked mountainous country in what was once the southernmost extension of the former Soviet Union. Only about 6% of the land is available for agricultural production.[18] The Khatlon Region in southern Tajikistan is key for agricultural production. Tajikistan's high vulnerability to climate change and natural disasters represents an additional challenge to successful economic management (Table 5). In 1992–2016, natural and climate-related disasters led to GDP losses of roughly $1.8 billion, affecting almost 7 million people.

Following sustained growth rates in the last decade, Tajikistan has achieved lower middle-income status, with a gross national income per capita of $1,240 for 2019 ($1,240 for 2015) (footnote 17). Tajikistan's growth in GDP was the highest among the five countries (Table 10). Even though Tajikistan's GDP per capita has been growing at a rate higher than that of its neighbors, GDP per capita is significantly below theirs.

Past growth performance was driven mainly by services and agriculture and supported by private consumption.[19] Since 2000, services, which remain dominated by domestic non-tradable subsectors with low productivity, have contributed almost 43% of GDP growth. Although industry's contribution to growth has risen in recent years,

---

[16] The World Bank. The World Bank in Tajikistan: Overview.
[17] World Bank. World Development Indicators (accessed October 2020).
[18] TajStat. 2015. *Tajikistan in Figures*. Dushanbe. According to ADB, a quarter of Tajikistan's total land area (14 million hectares) is agricultural land. In 2010, however, less than one-fifth of agricultural land was classified as arable.
[19] World Bank Group. 2019. *Tajikistan Country Economic Memorandum: Nurturing Tajikistan's Growth Potential: Macroeconomics, Trade and Investment Global Practice Europe and Central Asia Region*. Washington, DC.

agriculture remains the second-largest sector, contributing the bulk of employment, but also has the lowest productivity. Public and state-owned enterprises continue dominating industrial output, producing about 70% of the total. The private sector's role in the economy remains limited, contributing to only 13% of formal employment and 15% of total investments in 2018. On the demand side, private consumption was the main contributor to growth, especially before the 2014 resource price shock, when remittances peaked at nearly the equivalent of 45% of GDP. In 2015–2017, growth momentum was underpinned by a large public investment push, stretching fiscal balances to the limits of long-term sustainability.

The government's vision is expressed in the National Development Strategy up to 2030, which sets the overall direction of economic development. Several sector policies and programs cover social sectors such as education, vocational training, employment, migration, health, among others, as well as economic sectors such as tourism, agriculture, and energy.

Since 2011, the sector-wise composition of GDP has not changed significantly (Figure 2). With a share above 40%, services and trade remain the main contributors to GDP. The service sector's share of GDP has increased constantly since 1996. The contribution of industry and construction has moderately increased since 2010, while agriculture's share of GDP has been decreasing every year since independence in 1991. Reflecting Tajikistan's slow transition from a planned to a market economy, manufacturing has remained below 10% of GDP, which is low for a middle-income country.

Almost 700 SOEs still exist,[20] mainly in infrastructure and communal services, energy, communications, transport, trade, banking, insurance, and metal processing. They provide 30% of formal employment and are responsible for

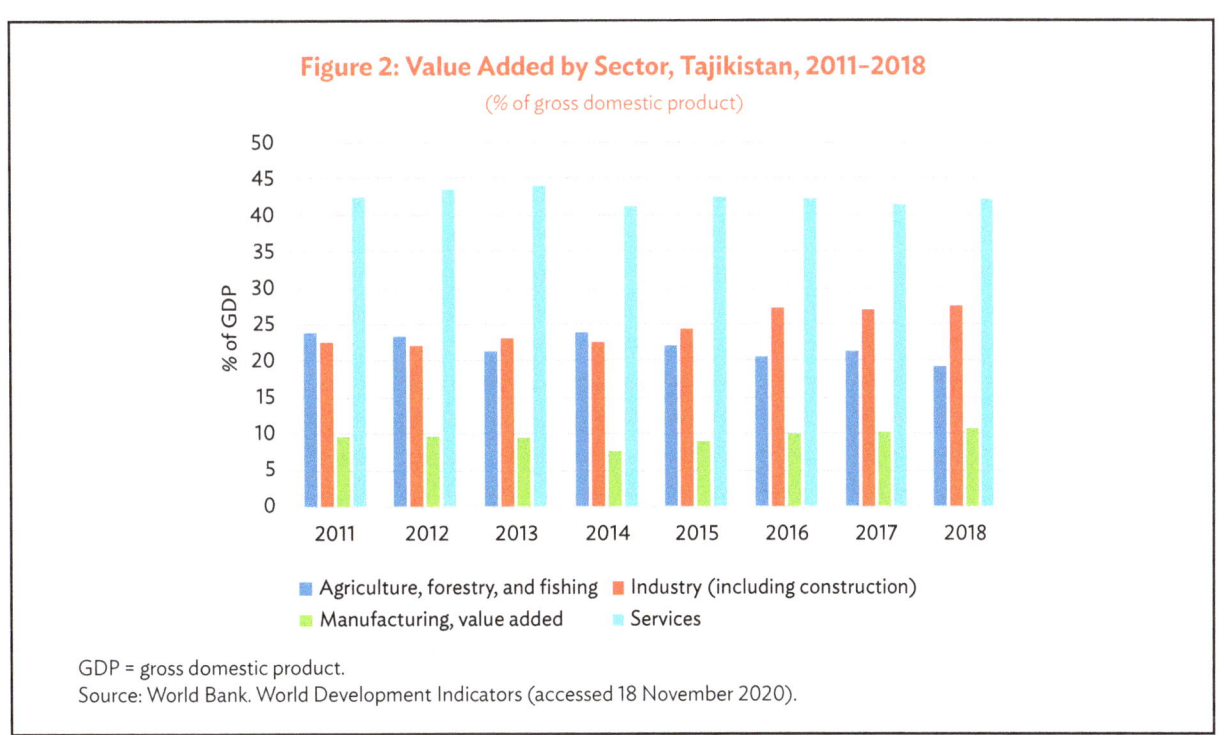

GDP = gross domestic product.
Source: World Bank. World Development Indicators (accessed 18 November 2020).

---

[20] In 2013, 687 SOEs were listed in the Registry of State-Owned Enterprises, but the Tax Administration reported 800. Only 31% of the total workforce is employed by private companies.

42% of total value added and 50% of total investment in fixed capital.[21] The 24 largest SOEs employ 51,370 workers. Most SOEs are characterized by overemployment and poor productivity.[22] In sectors where competition by private companies is allowed, the performance of SOEs is generally weaker than that of private enterprises (footnote 22).

SOEs—particularly the largest, including Tajik Aluminum Company (TALCO)[23]—show consistent operating losses and have accumulated substantial debt. The government had to spend almost $500 million in 2016 to bail out the banks that hold unpaid loans given to SOEs, among other issues.

Before the outbreak of the COVID-19 pandemic, international financial institutions forecast 2020 GDP growth rates for Tajikistan of 4.4% (World Bank) and 5.5% (ADB),[24] from the 7.5% economic growth rate recorded in 2019. It is too early to assess the medium-term effect of COVID-19, but preliminary estimates suggest that, at best, the economy will stagnate in 2020, with a risk of negative growth, depending on the duration and extent of the pandemic.

Human Resource Situation

Out of 189 countries, Tajikistan ranks 148th in GDP per capita (footnote 17) and 125th in the HDI (Table 6). Tajikistan's HDI value for 2018 is 0.656, which places the country in the medium human development category. In 1990–2018, Tajikistan's HDI value increased by 5.2% from 0.623 to 0.656. Table 16 reviews Tajikistan's progress in each HDI indicator. In 1990–2018, life expectancy at birth increased by 7.8 years, the mean years of schooling increased by 1.1 years, and expected years of schooling decreased by 0.8 years. Tajikistan's gross national income per capita decreased by about 13.8%.[25]

Table 16: Human Development Index, Tajikistan, 1990–2018

Year	Life Expectancy at Birth	Expected Years of Schooling	Mean Years of Schooling	GNI per Capita, 2011 (PPS $)	HDI Value
1990	63.1	12.0	9.6	4,029	0.623
1995	63.2	10.3	10.6	1,339	0.550
2000	65.5	9.7	10.6	1,246	0.550
2005	67.7	10.7	10.5	1,832	0.593
2010	69.6	11.1	10.9	2,696	0.634
2015	70.9	11.2	10.5	3,074	0.645
2016	71.1	11.2	10.5	3,164	0.647
2017	71.2	11.2	10.4	3,317	0.650
2018	70.9	11.4	10.7	3,482	0.656

GNI = gross national income, HDI = Human Development Index, PPS = purchasing power standard.
Source: United Nations Development Programme. 2019. Human Development Report.

---

[21] World Bank. 2014. *Fiscal Risks from State-Owned Enterprises. Policy Note.* Washington, DC.
[22] ADB. 2018. *State-Owned Enterprise Engagement and Reform. Thematic Evaluation.* Manila.
[23] TALCO benefits not only from state electricity subsidies but also from routine debt writes-offs. C. Putz. 2016. Tajikistan's Aluminum Company Lives on Subsidies and Debt Write-Offs. *The Diplomat.* 28 October.
[24] ADB. 2020. *Asian Development Outlook.* Manila; and World Bank. 2020. *Europe and Central Asia Economic Update.* Washington, DC.
[25] United Nations Development Programme. 2019. Human Development Report.

Table 17: Population in Multidimensional Poverty, Tajikistan, 2017
(%)

	Headcount Ratio: Population in Multidimensional Poverty	Intensity of Deprivation among the Poor	Vulnerable to Poverty (20.00%–33.32% intensity of deprivation)	In Severe Poverty (intensity higher than 50%)
	Population	Average of weighted deprivation	Population	Population
Turkmenistan	0.40	36.08	2.41	0.00
Kazakhstan	0.45	35.56	1.78	0.00
Kyrgyz Republic	2.28	36.32	8.31	0.04
Tajikistan	7.44	38.96	20.09	0.73

Source: Oxford Poverty and Human Development Initiative (OPHI). 2019. *Multidimensional Poverty Index Data Bank*. Oxford: OPHI, University of Oxford.

Tajikistan's 2018 HDI of 0.656 is above the average of 0.634 for countries in the medium human development group, below the average of 0.779 for Europe and Central Asia, and the lowest of the five Central Asian countries (Table 6).

Slow but sustained growth has not only contributed to a higher HDI score but also significantly reduced the share of the population living in poverty (Tables 9 and 17). In 1999, based on the living standards survey, 81% of the population was classified as poor. Based on the household budget survey, which factors seasonal changes, 47% of the population was classified as poor in 2009 and 35.6% in 2012. According to the World Bank, the poverty rate dropped from 43.8% in 2010 to 27.4% in 2018 (footnote 17).

Strong economic growth and rising wage income remain the primary drivers of poverty reduction. Therefore, maintaining robust economic growth and job creation will be crucial to further decreasing poverty. However, progress has been slower in reducing nonmonetary poverty. Recently available micro data suggest that limited or no access to education (secondary and tertiary), heating, and sanitation are the main contributors to nonmonetary poverty (footnote 17).

Economic Impact of COVID-19

Early assessments of the impact of COVID-19 suggest that the outbreak has caused severe disruptions in the labor market and sharply falling remittances from migrant workers abroad. In April 2020, President Emomali Rahmon reported to the International Monetary Fund (IMF) that remittances from the Russian Federation were reduced by 50% and that, in March, remittances were about $80 million less than 12 months before. The income of every fourth family in Tajikistan depends on labor migrants. According to official statistics, imports and exports fell sharply in May. Exports amounted to only $40 million, 56% less than in the same period the previous year. Imports amounted to only $195 million, 32% less than in the previous year. Experts estimate economic damage at $600 million. Transport, tourism, retail, and finance, in particular, have slowed down.[26]

---

[26] *ReliefWeb*. 2020. Impact of COVID-19 on Lives, Livelihoods and Micro, Small and Medium-Sized Enterprises (MSMEs) in Tajikistan. 1 October.

According to the World Bank, Tajikistan's economy, like other countries in the region, stagnated in 2020 following the COVID-19 outbreak and the closure of international borders. GDP growth is expected not to exceed 1% in 2020, reflecting the implications of the pandemic and the slowdown in the PRC and the Russian Federation. These implications include a sharp decline in trade and lower commodity prices, a likely large drop in remittances, and worsened prospects for transport and tourism. Growth will likely remain weak in 2021–2022, depending on the long-term development of the pandemic (footnote 26).

To mitigate the adverse impacts of COVID-19, the government launched the COVID-19 Country Preparedness and Response Plan and countercyclical measures. These include a health and social protection package to assist the poor and vulnerable, and economic measures to ensure food security and safeguard small businesses most at risk. Food security will be ensured through food price monitoring and controls and provision of agricultural inputs to farmers to increase production. Subsidized lending and tax relief will be extended to affected micro, small, and medium-sized enterprises, of which at least 24% are led by women.

International support to implement the measures has been massive. For instance, to mitigate the adverse economic and social impacts of the pandemic, under ADB's COVID-19 Active Response and Expenditure Support Program, Tajikistan has received a $50 million grant, including social assistance to at least 207,000 poor households and an additional one-time cash transfer.[27] The World Bank's assistance includes health equipment and training of healthcare staff as well as cash transfers to vulnerable households. The World Food Program has provided cash for work assistance. The World Health Organization has assisted with COVID-19 testing and tracing equipment and expertise. Other donors that have helped diminish the effects of the pandemic include the United States Agency for International Development, UNDP, the United Nations International Children's Emergency Fund, and the EU.

Labor Market Trends

Tajikistan's strong growth performance in the last decade has not translated into corresponding job creation to accommodate the rapid entry of young workers into the workforce. The 7.0% average annual GDP growth rate observed during 2009–2019 was accompanied by only a 1.1% annual increase in net jobs. The working-age population increased by about 3% per year during the same period.[28] This means that employment growth is 2.3 times slower than the growth of new entrants to the labor market. At the same time, the labor participation rate has been constantly decreasing, from 59% to 42%.[29] According to the World Bank, 11% of the labor force was without a job in 2019.[30] The unemployment rate is expected to increase significantly because of the COVID-19 pandemic.

Although agriculture accounts for not more than about 22% of GDP, it continues to provide employment and thus income for more than half of the population, reflecting low agricultural productivity.[31] The share of the population dependent on agriculture is much higher than in neighboring countries. Services and trade employ almost one-third of the population. Industry, including construction, demonstrates signs of accelerated growth, with double-digit growth rates since 2011, confirming that the government's effort to boost job creation, especially in industry, is starting to have an impact.

---

[27] ADB. 2020. ADB Approves Additional $2.5 Million Grant to Tajikistan for COVID-19 Response. News release. 7 August.
[28] World Bank Group. 2019. *Tajikistan Country Economic Memorandum: Nurturing Tajikistan's Growth Potential: Macroeconomics, Trade and Investment Global Practice Europe and Central Asia Region*. Washington, DC.
[29] TajStat. *Labor Force Survey (LFS) 2004 and 2016* (accessed 20 October 2020). Dushanbe.
[30] World Bank. 2020. Unemployment, Total (% of total labor force) (modeled ILO estimate). 20 September (accessed 7 October 2020).
[31] TajStat. 2017. *Labor Force Survey 2016*. Dushanbe.

Applying the ILO definition of the informal economy,[32] the TajStat Labor Force Survey (LFS) 2016 found that there were 133,359 people employed in the informal sector in Tajikistan in 2016, amounting to 15.7% of the total number of people employed in non-agriculture sectors. Of those employed in the informal sector, 106,354 were men and only 27,005 women; 30.9% reported being self-employed and 29.3% employed, 19.1% were recorded as employers, 11.3% were home workers in private households, and 5.8% were unpaid workers who helped family members. Compared with the LFS-2009 data, the proportion of employed people in the informal sector has declined by 33.3%, while the proportion of the total employed people in the formal sector has increased from 51.0% in 2009 to 84.3% in 2016.[33]

Women face a considerable disadvantage in employment. Although working-age females constitute more than half of the population, their participation rate in the labor force is 27.8% compared with 59.7% for men and is lower than that of other countries in the region (Table 11). Women are concentrated in a limited number of occupations, mainly "unskilled workers" (mostly in agriculture), "handymen," "cleaners and servants," textile workers, teachers, and market traders.[34] In addition, many women are involved in unpaid work for family businesses.[35] Women are also less likely to be self-employed (7% compared with 12% for men).

The low participation rate of women is partly attributable to their primary role of caring for children, as more than 75% of women are the primary caregiver. Low participation of women in the "official" workforce is indicative of their significant involvement in the informal economy and their low levels of formal qualification or training, which make them uncompetitive when applying for jobs.[36] Most of the economically inactive female population is 25–49 years old. The sharp decline in women's economic activity after this age corresponds directly to when they leave the labor market, marry, start families, and have increased household obligations. In addition to domestic task distribution inequalities, the generally lower level of education (especially vocational education) of women and their lack of professional qualifications and high fertility rate, combined with the absence of childcare facilities and gender stereotypes, place women in a weak employment position. Even among the working population, women are more commonly members of producers' cooperatives while men generally are employers or self-employed (as own-account workers).[37]

Youth (aged 15–24 years) who are idle (i.e., NEET) represent 40% of the total, which is high by regional standards.[38] In 2003–2013, NEET rates among youth increased from 37% to 41% despite relatively favorable economic conditions. The NEET rate for female youth is considerably higher than for male youth; in 2017, it was 52% for women and 30% for men. Youth NEETs are commonly considered "inactive" or "unproductive" when not looking for a job. However, a large proportion of NEETs, especially women, perform unpaid housework and produce nonmarket goods and services that are essential for household consumption and well-being.

---

[32] The ILO defines as informal those households or non-corporate enterprises that belong to households that produce goods and services for sale and do not have the status of a legal entity. Following the ILO's recommendations, the LFS excluded agriculture from the survey's calculation of employment in the informal sector.
[33] Several people the study team spoke to questioned the LFS finding. They argued that, when considering the number of new entrants to the labor force, the limited number of new job openings in the formal sector, and the decreasing number of labor migrants, it is difficult to believe that the number of people who depend on the informal economy for their living has declined. The World Bank study also contradicts this finding.
[34] Footnote 29, p. 41.
[35] World Bank. 2017. *Tajikistan: Addressing Challenges to Create More and Better Jobs.* February.
[36] M. Dermastia et al. 2017. *Value Chain Analysis of the Tourism Sector in Tajikistan.* Washington, DC. World Bank. p. 51. Family members account for 75% of the workforce in informal firms compared with 60% for formal firms. The share of family members in accommodation, food and beverage, and distribution nodes is roughly double for informal firms.
[37] ADB. 2016. *Tajikistan: Country Gender Assessment.* Manila.
[38] The estimate of the NEET rate varies between different sources, depending on the extent to which underemployed youth in the informal economy are included.

The low youth participation rates may explain why a large percentage of migrant workers are young men who use "nonofficial" ways of going abroad to find a job. In recent years, demand for construction workers in the Russian Federation has fallen. The young men, who are there illegally, have been among the first to be deported back to Tajikistan and, in many cases, barred from reentering the Russian Federation.

As to employment outcomes, women are at a disadvantage. In 2003–2018, the disparity between male and female employment rates increased. In 2003, the gap was 21 percentage points, increasing to 35 percentage points by 2018. Employed women work mostly in the public sector, while almost a quarter of women are also involved in unpaid work for family businesses, as opposed to 13% of men (footnote 35). Women are less likely to be self-employed (7% compared with 12% of men). The proportion of young people who do not work and do not study makes up 29.3% of the total number of youth (aged 15–29 years), of whom more than 88.1% are women.

In general, the level of vocational education of the employed population remains low. Only 29.8% of the workforce has professional education, reflecting the low level of industrialization, but that share is gradually changing. Data from three LFS surveys show that the proportion of employed people with secondary vocational education increased from 7.9% to 8.9% in 2004–2016, and the proportion of people with higher education increased from 11.2% to 17.0%. In the same period, the proportion of employed people with primary vocational education decreased from 7.5% to 3.9%. The analysis of the LFS-2016 data revealed a discrepancy between the level of education of the population aged 30–75 years and employment in the workplace, which showed that work performed by 50.2% of the employed adult population does not correspond to the level of education or acquired skills.[39]

Another significant change in Tajikistan's employment structure can be observed in the growth of private sector jobs and reduction of public sector jobs. In 2016, 66% of the employed population worked in the private sector. The formal private sector is squeezed between a large public sector and the informal sector and is not well developed. The officially hired workers in the private sector account for only 13% of total employment, and the share of potential entrepreneurs seeking to start their own business is extremely low, at only 11.8%, which indicates that entrepreneurs face obstacles in opening and running businesses. Most formal private sector firms are small and young, face difficulties, and are not motivated to expand (footnote 35).

Although the economy is undergoing structural changes because of the transition from agriculture and industry to services, current development does not sufficiently create jobs or reduce poverty. The 6.8% average annual growth rate observed during 2007–2017 was accompanied by only a 1.1% (23,364) annual increase in net jobs, while the working-age population increased by about 3.0% per year (1.2 million cumulative) (footnote 39). Employment growth is 2.3 times slower than the growth of labor resources. The labor participation rate has been constantly decreasing, from 58.6% to 42.4% (footnote 29). The growth elasticity of employment fell from 0.33 in 2000–2009 to just 0.13 in 2010–2014. Similarly, the 40% cumulative economic growth recorded during 2013–2017 was accompanied by only a modest decline in the poverty rate, from 34.3% in 2013 to 29.5% in 2017, reflecting the low growth elasticity of poverty reduction (footnote 39).

Several recent studies have discussed possible initiatives to diversify the economy to improve the role of the private sector and create jobs. The studies revolve around two issues: (i) ways to improve the business climate and (ii) strategies for tapping export potential. For instance, according to ADB, "Tajikistan will reap significant economic dividends by strengthening its information technology infrastructure—making internet access cheaper and better and encouraging private investment in data and voice services—and by strengthening training of the youth."[40] Furthermore, the ADB's *Asian Development Outlook 2019* states: "Tajikistan should

---

[39] Statistics Agency under the President of the Republic of Tajikistan. 2017. *Situation in the Labour Market in the Republic of Tajikistan.* Based on the results of the LFS-2016, Dushanbe, pp. 30–47.
[40] ADB. 2019. *Asian Development Outlook 2019.* Manila.

explore opportunities to export products for which it enjoys a comparative advantage, such as high-value agricultural products. Giving farmers technical support in marketing and establishing marketing associations to attain economies of scale and reduce transaction costs could help boost production, sales, and ultimately exports, which would raise rural incomes" (footnote 40). The report highlights the need to tackle shortcomings in the investment climate, such as complex procedures for starting a business, and costly customs, transport and logistic procedures, combined with weak access to credit and tax administration, which discourage private investors.

Labor Migration

In 2018, based on data submitted by local migration offices, the government reported that almost half a million working-age people or about 10% of the labor force had left Tajikistan in search of employment abroad. Several studies have challenged this number, stating that the actual number is significantly higher. For instance, the Japan International Cooperation Agency (JICA) estimated that there were 780,829 migrant workers in 2018, corresponding to 14% of the labor force.[41] The Russian Federation is by far the preferred destination for migration. Among other things, the recently launched ADB Tajikistan Skills and Employability Enhancement Project will better prepare migrants for the Russian Federation labor market by imparting vocational skills and information about rules and procedures.

Since 2014, the flow of labor migrants to the Russian Federation has decreased because of its difficult economic situation and the legislative changes that have made it more difficult and more expensive for migrants to work there legally. According to the Migration Services of Ministry of Labor, Migration and Employment, as of September 2019, the list of Tajik citizens banned from working in the Russian Federation has grown by about 20,000 every 3 months. According to Ministry of Labor, Migration and Employment, as of September 2019 more than 200,000 Tajik citizens were banned from reentering the Russian Federation.

Most labor migrants are male (86.7%) (Table 18). The largest group of migrants is aged 15–29 years (45.4%), followed by the group aged 30–44 years (39.5%).[42] More than 85% of labor migrants are from rural areas. Most migrants were unemployed before migrating. Roughly 75% of migration is seasonal, meaning that migrants return to Tajikistan at least once a year.[43]

Table 18: Number of Tajikistan Migrant Workers by Gender, 2015–2018

Year	2015	2016	2017	2018
Total number of migrants	551,728	517,308	487,757	484,176
Number and %, males	487,137	435,457	419,721	419,664
	88.3%	84.2%	86.1%	86.7%
Number and %, females	64,591	81,851	68,036	64,512
	11.7%	15.8%	13.9%	13.3%

Source: TajStat. 2018. *Labor Market in Republic of Tajikistan*. Dushanbe (accessed 2 November 2020).

---

[41] JICA. 2018. *Migration, Living Conditions and Skills: Panel Study, Tajikistan Survey.* Dushanbe.
[42] TajStat. *Labor Force Survey 2019.* Dushanbe (accessed 1 November 2020).
[43] *European Training Foundation Migration Survey, 2010, p. 23.* Torino.

Table 19: Distribution of Tajikistan Migrants Working in the Russian Federation, by Industry

Industry	Men (%)	Women (%)	Total (%)
Construction	65	11	59
Wholesale, retail trade, hotels, and restaurants	13	54	17
Manufacturing	5	4	5
Transport, storage, communication	6	2	5
Other communal and personal services	4	14	5
Agriculture, hunting, fishing, forestry	4	3	4
Education	0.5	4	1
Health and social services	0.5	3	1
Public administration and defense	1	3	1
Others	2	2	2

Source: TajStat. 2010. *Migration Survey*. Dushanbe (accessed 30 October 2020).

The Russian Federation is the main destination for labor migration (98.7%) (footnote 42). Most migrant male workers find employment in construction, mostly as unskilled laborers, while most female migrants find work in the services sector (Table 19). Most male migrants come from rural areas.

Few migrants have any qualifications beyond completed secondary school. According to the LFS-2016, 72% of migrants have completed secondary education (grade 11); for 12%, the highest level was grade 9. Those with professional qualifications, i.e., initial vocational education and training (IVET), secondary vocational, or higher vocational and technical education, constituted only 15% of migrants (Table 20).

Ministry of Labor, Migration and Employment has developed various support measures and advisory structures for migrant workers. However, the measures either often fail to reach the target group, are ineffective, or do not reflect what is required. The urgency of such support measures has been greatly exacerbated by the COVID-19 pandemic. Deutsche Gesellschaft für Internationale Zusammenarbeit GmbH (GIZ), therefore, recently launched a project supporting Ministry of Labor, Migration and Employment's activities to reintegrate migrant workers into the domestic labor market. The project works with the private sector in setting up viable local self-help models.

Table 20: Level of Education of External Labor Migrants

Level of Education	Number	%
Postgraduate education (including resident postgraduate students)	315	0.1
Higher vocational and technical education	37,214	6.7
Secondary technical and vocational education and training	30,787	5.6
Initial vocational education and training	15,237	2.8
Secondary general education	397,991	71.9
Secondary basic education	68,932	12.4
No basic education	3,393	0.6
Total	**553,869**	**100.0**

Source: TajStat. 2016. *Labor Force Survey*. Dushanbe (accessed 15 October 2020).

Research has shown that as many as 80% of the migrants banned from reentry to the Russian Federation did not know about the ban when they left the country. Many found out about it only when they were turned away by Russian Federation border guards as there is no regular mechanism to inform "offenders" about their situation. In most cases, violation of Russian Federation migration procedures because of insufficient understanding triggered the reentry ban, but there are reports about working migrants who deliberately tried to stay under the authorities' radar by pretending to be tourists. At times, simple traffic violations and basic breaches of the law have resulted in a reentry ban.

Many returning migrants have trouble finding a suitable job because of poor job opportunities in their home country and because skills acquired abroad are either not relevant to the labor market or not acknowledged. An International Organization for Migration study on migrants banned from returning to the Russian Federation found that some 24% stated that their families had difficulty affording food and 33% said that, although their income is sufficient for food, it hardly allowed them to buy clothes and other daily necessities.[44]

B. Other Central Asian Countries

Kazakhstan

Macroeconomic Overview

The economy of Kazakhstan is the largest in Central Asia in absolute and per capita terms.[45] The breakup of the Soviet Union and the collapse of demand for Kazakhstan's traditional heavy industry products resulted in a sharp decline of the economy, with the steepest annual decline occurring in 1994. In 1995–1997, the pace of the government program of economic reform and privatization quickened, resulting in substantial shifting of assets to the private sector. Kazakhstan was granted "market economy country" status by the EU in 2000 and the United States in 2002.

While GDP per capita shrank by 25% in the 1990s, the economy has grown significantly since 2000, aided by increased world prices for leading exports: oil, metals, and grain. Business with the Russian Federation, the PRC, and neighboring CIS nations has helped propel growth.

Windfall revenues from the export of oil, gas, and other commodities, together with structural reforms, lifted Kazakhstan to upper-middle-income status in 2006. Today, the country is a major economic and political power in Central Asia. The quality of life of the average citizen improved significantly during the past 2 decades as incomes rose and unemployment rates dropped. Nonetheless, Kazakhstan continues to struggle to diversify its economy, strengthen its institutions, and balance regional disparities between its few economic centers and a vast periphery, where public services remain scarce and of poor quality. The economy remains heavily dependent on hydrocarbons and largely driven by capital-intensive extractive industries. Over the past 25 years, agriculture and manufacturing outputs have been declining as a share of GDP, employment, and exports, with jobs mostly created in the service sector.

Excessive reliance on commodity exports has made the economy vulnerable to external shocks. GDP growth slowed significantly because of lower commodity prices following the 2008 global financial crisis. A similar trend followed

---

[44] International Organization for Migration. 2014. *Tajik Migrants with Re-entry Bans to the Russian Federation*. Dushanbe.
[45] The section is based on ADB. 2017. *Country Partnership Strategy. Kazakhstan, 2017–2021: Promoting Economic Diversification, Inclusive Development, and Sustainable Growth*. Manila.

the oil price plunge and the slowdown of the economies of major trading partners in 2014, when the shortfall in export revenues reduced inflows to the National Fund, diminished budget revenues, lowered investments, and increased pressure on the exchange rate. The prolonged impact of these external economic shocks substantially affects the earlier results achieved in economic development and inclusiveness.

One of the main challenges faced by the government is to create a competitive manufacturing sector. Manufacturing has been unable to drive productivity and employment growth. Similarly, diversification of the tertiary sector toward sophisticated services with high export potential is yet to occur on a significant scale. Extractive industries amount to about 30% of GDP and contribute almost half of budget revenues and more than two-thirds of exports. The share of processed food in total exports was only 0.83% in 2015. Increased agricultural production would help utilize existing food-processing capacities and increase the non-oil value added in processing.

Despite some early privatization efforts, SOEs still dominate the economy in a variety of sectors. The companies are large and lack incentives to continue to improve the quality and efficiency of their services and products, while often keeping tariffs and prices below cost-recovery levels. These factors deter innovation and private sector participation in the economy, especially of small and medium-sized enterprises.

Since 2000, Kazakhstan has made impressive progress in reducing poverty and building a middle class. The economy grew at an average annual rate of 6.9% in 2001–2019.[46] The poverty rate dropped from 55% of the population in 2006 to less than 10% in 2018 as the middle class grew from 10% to more than 25%. Improvements in economic well-being were mainly the result of income gains from wage employment. In 2006–2019, Kazakhstan created about 1.3 million jobs in a labor force of 9.1 million people (in 2019), well above the increase in the working-age population.

According to a 2019 report by Kazakhstan's National Academy of Sciences, which cites data from the CIS's statistics committee, the "non-observed economy" (the informal sector) was equivalent to 22%–27% of the economy. The IMF, however, has found that the informal economy accounts for as much as 39% of GDP.[47]

Impact of COVID-19

According to the World Bank, the COVID-19 pandemic is the biggest shock to the economy in almost 2 decades and is already having a highly negative impact on growth.[48] While the collapse in oil prices in 2009 and 2015 shrank aggregated demand and rocked financial stability, the current crisis means that the supply side of the economy is affected by the series of lockdowns.

The government acted early to contain the spread of COVID-19. Following the announcement of a state of emergency, the government imposed quarantine control and provided support to those whose livelihoods were affected by the pandemic or by the emergency restrictions. The authorities introduced a fiscal package to support firms and households affected by the crisis.

GDP is projected to contract by 3.0% in 2020 and recover only modestly, by 2.5% in 2021. The current account deficit is expected to widen to above 5% of GDP in 2020, in large part owing to deteriorated terms of trade and decline in volume of oil exports.

---

[46] World Bank. GDP Growth (annual %) – Kazakhstan (accessed 28 October 2020).
[47] S. Bhutia. 2020. Measuring Central Asia's Shadow Economies. *eurasianetwork*. 21 February.
[48] World Bank. 2020. *Navigating the Crisis. Kazakhstan Economic Update*. Washington, DC.

A prolonged crisis is likely to increase poverty and inequality. Preliminary estimates suggest that the poverty rate might rise in 2020 from a projected 8.3% to 12.7%: equating to more than 800,000 additional people living in poverty.

The shock to the labor market by the pandemic and the mitigation measures has severe implications for employment, particularly in sectors that employ low-skilled workers. Unequal access to quality education, especially during lockdown, can negatively impact human capital development for the poor.

Labor Market Trends

According to the Statistics Committee of the Ministry of National Economy, youth (aged 15–28 years) make up about a quarter of the economically active population. However, youth unemployment is gradually decreasing and, in 2018, it was 3.9%. The level of long-term youth unemployment decreased from 2.4% in 2014 to 2.1% in 2018. Detailed data are not yet available, but preliminary observations from other countries show that young people are especially likely to lose their jobs as a result of the pandemic.[49]

Since 2011, Kazakhstan has consistently recorded low unemployment rates (below 5.0%) with more than a quarter of the employed being self-employed. Participation of the working-age population in the labor force is 77%. In 2018, the unemployment rate was just 5.6% for women and 4.2% for men (Table 9), while labor force participation was relatively high, at 65.3% for women and 77.1% for men (Table 8). While women participate less than men, the share of women participating in the labor force is high by international standards. In the decade through 2013 (just before the decline in oil prices in 2014), average real wages rose 7.7% annually. These labor market gains were the main drivers of large-scale poverty reduction and more inclusive growth. Earnings of the poorest 20% of households grew 90% in 2006–2015, with labor earnings accounting for more than three-quarters of the growth. However, the growth model led to job creation that was concentrated in low-productivity non-tradable service sectors. Kazakhstan experienced significant structural transformation in 2001–2019, with low-productivity agriculture shedding jobs and the resulting reallocation of employment contributing to productivity growth. The largest job-creating sectors included public services such as education, health, and other social services, along with construction, trade, and transport and storage in the private sector.

However, the youth segment, like the general labor market, remains unbalanced. First, young professionals are predominantly employed in the low-productivity industries. Thus, in 2018, 16.7% of employed youth worked in trade, 14.2% in agriculture, and 11.1% in education. Second, entrepreneurship remains unattractive for young people. An overwhelming proportion of employed youth are hired workers. Only 23.9% are self-employed. Third, 42.9% of employed young people have higher and incomplete higher education, while only 25.2% of the self-employed youth have higher education. Fourth, according to the Committee on Statistics, the average monthly nominal wage of working youth is only two-thirds the average monthly nominal wage. The lowest earnings are in agriculture, health care, and public administration.

In Central Asia, an important factor hindering the employment of young people is the gap between their professional orientation and the needs of enterprises. Employment among young people outside their specialty and employment of young graduates in jobs that do not require a high level of education tend to be widespread. According to statistics, the expected graduation rate of students (universities and colleges) in 2013–2018 was three times higher than expected demand for additional new workers (including vacancies). Another critical factor concerns young people's aspirations and incentives to work. Because of high salary expectations and self-esteem,

---

[49] This and the following paragraphs are based on A. Alshanskaya. 2019. *Youth Labor Market in Kazakhstan: Who Is in Demand and Who Is Left on the Sidelines?*. CABAR.asia. 5 July.

some young people might refuse to be employed. They do not consider entrepreneurship attractive. According to a study by the Youth Research Center, only 16.5% of those interviewed mentioned that they would like to start their own business within the next 3 years, while 51.0% said they did not plan to engage in business.

According to the Committee on Statistics of the Ministry of National Economy, 18.7% of unemployed young people searched for work for 6–12 months and 23.3% for 3–6 months, which might push them to look for informal work.

The share of NEET individuals is low in all age cohorts, including among youth, except for those aged 60–64 years as they retire. The NEET group makes up 7% of all young people.

Labor Migration

Kazakhstan has gone from being a sender to a receiver of migrant workers. The tipping point occurred in 2010–2015.[50] Until at least the mid-2000s, Kazakhstan, like other Central Asian states, experienced a net outflow of migrants. In recent years, however, it has registered more people coming than going.

The change is fueled by the oil-driven economic boom during the last decade. There has been an increasing demand for high-skilled labor in industry, business, and education, and for low-skilled labor in agriculture, bazaars, and construction. The Government of Kazakhstan has been more accommodating toward labor migrants, resulting in increased numbers of workers from the Kyrgyz Republic, Tajikistan, and Uzbekistan over the last few years. Remittances sent from Kazakhstan in 2017–2018 substantially increased. Uzbekistan has become the biggest exporter of labor to Kazakhstan (footnote 50).

Kazakhstan is home to an estimated more than 3.5 million migrants, more than half of whom crossed the border illegally. Many of the illegal migrants are working in small and medium-sized businesses. The lockdown caused by the COVID-19 outbreak has allegedly hit this group particularly hard.

Kyrgyz Republic

Macroeconomic Overview

Since gaining independence from the Soviet Union in 1991, the Kyrgyz Republic has experienced considerable political turbulence, accompanied by economic and social fragility, episodes of social unrest, and frequent changes of government. Although a certain level of stability has been established, several serious challenges persist, such as the urban–rural divide and continuing regional disparities, youth unemployment and marginalization, and the growing specter of religious radicalization. In view of these pressures, the government is placing high priority on regional and territorial development—a key focus of its medium-term development program—and improved governance. The government is seeking to improve relations with neighbors, especially Uzbekistan, with the expectation that greater regional cooperation, connectivity, and trade (including in energy and water) could boost growth and reduce social tensions.[51]

After a decade of serious economic decline, the economy grew at a robust pace in 2000–2016. The main drivers of economic growth have been gold extraction and worker remittance-fueled consumption. This growth model has enabled the economy to grow at an average annual rate of 4.2% in 2000–2019. However, growth has been highly volatile because of the limited diversification of the economy. One gold mine, Kumtor, accounts for about

---

[50] K. Sharifzoda. 2019. Why Is Kazakhstan a Growing Destination for Central Asian Migrant Workers? *The Diplomat*. 13 June.
[51] World Bank. 2018. *Kyrgyz Republic: From Vulnerability to Prosperity Systematic Country Diagnostic*. Washington, DC.

8% of GDP, while personal remittances accounted for 28.5% of GDP in 2019.[52] Despite moderate and volatile growth and stagnant non-gold industries, the structure of the economy has been changing. During 2000–2016, the share of agriculture declined from 36.6% to 14.4%, industry marginally increased from 25.8% (average in 2000–2004) to 27.7% (average in 2012–2016), and services expanded from 32.1% to 57.3%, with wholesale trade, retail trade, transport, and education as key segments. These changes reflect a long process of deindustrialization, as evidenced by declining traditional manufacturing and a failure to diversify into products or services embodying higher technological content.

Despite economic growth, the share of the population living below the international poverty line remains relatively high at 22.4% (2018) (Table 8). A still larger proportion of households are clustered just above the poverty line, making them vulnerable to poverty in the face of even small shocks, such as food price increases.

According to the World Bank, economic growth slowed significantly to 1.5% in the first quarter of 2020, down from 5.2% in the same period of 2019, as economic activity was hit by the COVID-19 outbreak and declining growth in the gold sector. Remittances are estimated to have declined by 11.5% in 2019 (footnote 50). "Full-year real GDP growth is projected to decline to 0.4% in 2020 due to the impact of the COVID-19 outbreak and the weakening growth in Russia. Gold production is expected to remain at the same level as in 2019, as the reduction at the Kumtor gold mine will be offset by a new gold project, Djerooi. Assuming that the outbreak is contained by the second half of 2020, GDP growth is forecast to rebound to 3.5% in 2021 and 4.6% in 2022."[53]

In 2020, the mean age of the population was 26.0 years (Table 1), making it the second youngest population in Central Asia, after Tajikistan, while the number of economically active people reached 2,547,400 or 40.6% of the total population.

Impact of COVID-19

The COVID-19 pandemic and measures to contain it have caused joblessness and domestic violence to spike, with GDP expected to sink by 10% in 2020, according to a new study by the UNDP, ADB, and the Kyrgyz Economic Policy Research Institute.[54]

Vital remittance inflows to the country could plunge by 25%, while unemployment could surge to 21%. Women, children, and vulnerable people such as those working without social protection in the informal economy have been hit hardest. From January to March, the number of reported domestic violence cases rose by an alarming 65% compared with the same period a year earlier.

Private spending on nonfood items and services has also plummeted, with a 15% drop in the volume of retail trade during the first half of 2020 and a 5.3% decline in GDP from January to June. Receipts from tourism and travel services are expected to drop 90% (footnote 54).

Labor Market Trends

The share of employment in agriculture fell from 53.1% in 2000 to 21.2% in 2019. Labor released from agriculture either emigrated to low-skilled jobs abroad or moved to informal jobs within the country. Agriculture retains a high proportion of self-employed workers (67% of all self-employed women and 53.8% men). Although industry's share of employment more than doubled from 10.5% in 2000 to 24.1% in 2019, it has grown slowly since 2007 when it

---
[52] World Bank. Personal Remittances, Received (% of GDP) – Kyrgyz Republic.
[53] World Bank. 2020. *Kyrgyz Republic Economic Outlook*.
[54] UNDP. 2020. *Kyrgyz Republic Could See GDP Plunge 10% as a Result of COVID-19, as Domestic Violence Surges*. 18 August.

first reached 20.0%. The employment share of manufacturing (within industry) fell from 8.3% in 2007 to 7.4% in 2015. The share of employment in services grew from 36.5% in 2000 to 54.8% in 2019. A significant proportion of the economy is in the informal sector, outside the government's control. Female labor participation fell from 60.1% in 2000 to 48.1% in 2019 because of the gradual erosion of previous state support mechanisms. The male labor force participation rate was 75.8% and the female rate 48.0% in 2018 (Table 8).[55]

A recent World Bank report highlights four challenges for the labor market: job creation, productivity, quality, and inclusion: "Job creation is currently not keeping pace with population growth. Each year, an estimated 50,000 individuals enter the labor market. By 2030, an estimated 4.6 million adults will be of working age. However, between 2009 and 2013 the workforce grew by an estimated 2% per annum, but the annual job creation only averaged 0.9%. Although wages have increased significantly, growth in labor productivity is relatively low for the region at 4.3% per annum. Increased informality in the service and industry sectors contribute to low productivity growth... Job quality is also a concern for further economic growth. Less than one-third of workers are employed in the formal sector. Of those in the formal sector, 60% are employed in the public sector. Formal, private sector employment is limited to a few sectors and is highly concentrated in urban areas. The labor market, therefore, consists of high rates of informality, as well as temporary, occasional, and seasonal work. Overall, the informal sector accounts for an estimated 20% of GDP. Job inclusivity is also an important challenge for the Kyrgyz Republic. One-third of working-age adults are not in the workforce... In 2018, approximately 38% of youth were active in the labor force. Although youth and women are the largest groups of potential workers, many are prevented from entering the labor force by social norms and structural constraints. Moreover, jobs tend to be regionally concentrated, with 66% and 53% of workers in Bishkek and Jalal-Abad, respectively, likely to have regularly paid employment, compared to 35% of workers in other regions... Overall, these challenges can be addressed through a combination of job growth, skilled labor force development, and labor equilibrating policies."[56]

Labor Migration

The Kyrgyz Republic considers labor migration as a tool to provide employment to surplus labor. According to a report of the State Migration Service, in 2017 more than 700,000 citizens of the Kyrgyz Republic were labor migrants, of whom most were in the Russian Federation and Kazakhstan.[57] The accession of the Kyrgyz Republic to the Eurasian Economic Union in 2015 significantly influenced the growth in the number of workers migrating from the Kyrgyz Republic to the Russian Federation: from 526,000 in 2014 to about 665,000 in 2017. The eased access has also led to a decrease in the number of reentry-banned migrants to the Russian Federation, which was estimated to be 83,000 in 2017 compared with 118,000 in 2016. Remittances of labor migrants have been progressively increasing. In 2018, they made up to 33.2% of GDP (Table 9), the second highest in the world. The outflow of labor results in wage growth for workers remaining in the country, which has increased faster than economic growth.[58]

Regarding age determination of migrants working abroad, according to statistics 60.46% of the total number of migrants are aged 15–29 years. Almost 40% of the Kyrgyz Republic migrants to the Russian Federation are women. They work primarily in services, catering, textiles, and domestic work. Most women migrants work in informal employment for more than 10 hours a day and have limited access to social protection services. Women migrants often face multiple forms of discrimination and stigma in the country of origin and destination and become vulnerable to sexual and gender-based violence.

---

[55] ADB. 2018. *Country Partnership Strategy: Kyrgyz Republic 2018–2022*. Manila. Data are updated based on the World Bank databank.
[56] World Bank. 2020. *Building the Right Skills for Human Capital Education, Skills, and Productivity in the Kyrgyz Republic*. Washington, DC.
[57] Other sources estimate a significantly higher number of labor migrants.
[58] International Organization for Migration. 2018. Current Migration Situation and Trends in Kyrgyzstan. Dushanbe.

Most migrant workers have completed general secondary education and take up semiskilled occupations abroad, especially in construction, agriculture, and services.

Turkmenistan

Macroeconomic Overview

The economy is largely reliant on the extraction and exploitation of natural resources such as natural gas and petroleum. Experts estimate that Turkmenistan is home to the fourth-largest natural gas reserve in the world. Since the early 2000s, the country has maintained relatively consistent growth in the gas industry.

"With growth averaging 11% annually since 2007, according to official data, Turkmenistan remains one of the fastest growing economies in the world. Abundant hydrocarbon resources and high international commodity prices helped Turkmenistan achieve upper middle-income status in 2011. While other sectors' contributions to GDP are gradually increasing, growth is still driven largely by hydrocarbons, including related gas processing and oil refining, and indirectly by high public investment. The state plays a leading role in most aspects of the economy—mainly through its financing of extractive industries, which account for over 35% of GDP and 80% of public investment, but only 14% of employment."[59] However, real GDP growth weakened slightly in 2018, slowing to 6.2% from 6.5% in 2017, reflecting a decline in the non-hydrocarbon economy. Net exports positively contributed to economic growth, but the growth was more than offset by weakened domestic demand, which reflected a decline in public investment to 22% of GDP in 2018 from an average of 30% in 2014–2017.[60]

Because of weaker demand for gas and oil products from key trading partners, economic growth for 2020 is expected to be extremely modest, with growth of 4%–5% in 2021. Turkmenistan does not release official statistics on living standards, and little is known about the country's labor market.

"Tight administrative controls and the public sector's dominant role in economic activity have hindered private sector development. Despite the growth of the private sector's share in segments of the economy, public sector and state-owned monopolies continue to govern the economy and the formal labor market. Apart from the hydrocarbon sector, foreign direct investment remains limited" (footnote 60). The private sector dominates in agriculture (60%), trade (70%), and transport (56%).

Impact of COVID-19

The effect of the COVID-19 pandemic in Turkmenistan is unknown, as the government insists no cases have been recorded.

Labor Market Trends

As pointed out by the World Bank, data constraints prevent a thorough analysis of the labor market and, thus, the social impact of slower economic growth (footnote 60). The following analysis is, therefore, confined to general observations regarding labor market trends.

According to official statistics, industry is the largest contributor to GDP, at 49%, although it employs only about 14% of the total labor force. The gas and oil industry is the main source of employment. Construction is categorized

---

[59] World Bank Group. 2015. *Joint Country Engagement Note for Turkmenistan for the Period FY16–FY17.* Washington, DC.
[60] World Bank. 2020. *Economic Outlook Turkmenistan.* Washington, DC.

within industry although it primarily survives because of government contracts. Although most of the country is desert, agriculture (which relies heavily on irrigation) accounts for almost 8% of GDP and continues to employ nearly half of the workforce.[61] Services employ 38% of the labor force and contribute 38% of GDP. The sector includes a large variety of businesses, including hospitality, tourism, retail, health care, communications, customer service, financial services, and banking institutions. Most services are under government control, particularly banking and financial services. Because of the focus on government, 95% of lines of credit are issued to government institutions rather than to the public.

Except for finance and education, where most employees have higher education qualifications, and health care, where most have secondary professional qualifications, the labor force lacks qualifications beyond the 12-year general secondary education.

The government's investment in industrial production, particularly processing, and the massive state-financed construction programs have increased demand for specialized professionals.[62] The oil and gas industry is another major source of employment for specialized professions.

The challenge for the government is to equip the growing labor force (40% of its population is below 25 years of age) with the competencies required for a knowledge society. A persistent lack of professional skills would jeopardize the government's plans to diversify the economy beyond hydrocarbons.

Data on unemployment are sensitive. Official sources set it at 3.4% (official statistics record only those who are registered by the Employment Service as jobless), while other sources estimate the de facto unemployment rate to be far higher; some sources set it as high as 50% of the labor force.[63]

Youth unemployment has received little official attention. However, in May 2019, the government presented a program for youth adaptation to the changing labor market and employment improvement. The program is intended "to review the demand for specialists by industry, improving the professional qualification of youth, creating decent living conditions for young professionals and encouraging their employment." The same month, the President instructed relevant authorities to set up new manufacturing facilities and create jobs for inhabitants of Ashgabat's new residential neighborhoods (footnote 63).

Labor Migration

A substantial but unknown number of young people from Turkmenistan migrate to other countries in the region. Some do so to continue their education, others to search for employment. Turkey is an especially popular destination, but many go to Kazakhstan and the Russian Federation. The Turkmenistan authorities have an ambiguous attitude toward migrants. The government has emphasized several times citizens' right to seek employment outside of the country but also continues to create more and more obstacles to stop groups of residents attempting to leave; returning migrants are frequently harassed.[64] There are no official statistics of Turkmenistan citizens living abroad, but unofficial sources estimate that in Turkey alone there are several hundred thousand workers from Turkmenistan. Another source suggests that almost 2 million citizens live outside of Turkmenistan.

---

[61] This and the two following paragraphs are based on A. Pariona. 2019. The Biggest Industries in Turkmenistan. *World Atlas*. 12 June.
[62] ADB. 2020. *Asian Development Bank and Turkmenistan: Fact Sheet*. October.
[63] *The Chronicle of Turkmenistan*. 2019. 25 May.
[64] V. Volkov. 2018. Why Do the Authorities of Turkmenistan Create Obstacles for Their Migrant Workers? *Deutsche Welle*. 9 July.

Uzbekistan

Macroeconomic Overview

With gigantic power generation facilities from the Soviet era and an ample supply of natural gas, Uzbekistan has become the largest electricity producer in Central Asia. Renewable energy constitutes more than 23% of the energy sector. The national Uzbekneftegas is among the biggest producers of natural gas in the world. The country has significant untapped reserves of oil and gas.[65]

Uzbekistan embarked on the path to market-oriented economic reforms later than other members of the former Soviet Union. Until recently, the country remained a closed, centrally-planned economy, with growth largely driven by commodity export revenues that financed import substitution industrialization. Such growth was achieved through import barriers and restrictions to capital outflows, which supported a wide network of SOEs and a few private sector participants.

Following the global economic crisis in 2014, it became increasingly evident that economic growth was not accompanied by productivity growth or sufficient high-quality job creation, leading to substantial outward labor migration. In 2017, the country launched an ambitious and unprecedented program of market-oriented reforms. With the drivers of the old growth model exhausted, the new leadership embarked on a strong program of market reforms.

The 2017–2021 strategic plan includes reforming the bureaucracy; establishing the rule of law; opening the economy; and promoting education, health, and infrastructure to attract private investments and reduce unemployment and poverty. The government aims to transform Uzbekistan into an industrialized, upper-middle-income country by 2030 and recently announced plans to modernize agriculture, reduce government ownership of state-owned assets and enterprises, and loosen constraints on financial markets.

The reforms have led to a surge in investment, and a pickup in consumption boosted GDP growth to 5.6% in 2019 from 4.7% in 2017. Public investment in industrial facilities; infrastructure (gas, hydroelectricity, roads, and housing); and household consumption (more than 50% of GDP) promoted growth. Abundant and varied natural resources, low public debt, solid foreign exchange reserves, aggressive investment programs, a growing labor force, and a strategic geographic position between the PRC and Europe further factor into economic development.

Impact of COVID-19

The COVID-19 pandemic and measures to contain it have hit Uzbekistan hard, cutting exports and remittances, straining the government coffers, and forcing most small businesses across the country to close. Exports dropped 18% in the first quarter compared with the same period a year earlier, the government reports, while 475,000 or 85% of small businesses were forced to close in March 2020. The share of households with at least one member actively working fell more than 40 percentage points, from 85% to 43%, from March to April 2020. Among the self-employed, income fell 67%, according to the World Bank.[66]

According to the updated IMF forecasts from April 2020, because of the outbreak of COVID-19, GDP growth is expected to slow down to 1.8% in 2020 and pick up to 7.0% in 2021, subject to the post-pandemic global economic recovery.

---

[65] This section is based on World Bank. Uzbekistan Overview; and ADB. 2020. *Uzbekistan: Country Operations Business Plan 2021–2023*. Manila.
[66] UNDP. 2020. Uzbekistan's Health Care System, Economy Hit Hard by COVID-19. 6 July.

Labor Market Trends

The workforce is 15.5 million out the 33.0 million population. Agriculture plays a major role, accounting for 28.7% of GDP and employing 33.1% of the total workforce. Industry accounts for 28.4% of GDP and employs 30.3% of the total workforce. Uzbekistan is the main producer of machinery and heavy equipment in Central Asia. The country manufactures machines and equipment for cotton cultivation, harvesting, and processing, and for use in the textile industry, irrigation, and road construction. Services account for 31.6% of GDP and employ 36.4% of the total workforce. Key services include transport and tourism. Uzbekistan was the fourth fastest-growing country for tourism in 2019 (+27.3%), receiving 6.7 million tourists.[67] Out of 15.5 million people employed in the labor market, more than 8 million are in the informal sector, including 2.6 million labor migrants.

The official unemployment rate was reported at 6.1% in 2019; unemployment of youth (aged 15–24 years) was reported at 12.0%.[68] According to the World Bank, the reports severely underestimate the extent of underemployment as indicated by the size of the informal sector. It constitutes 42% of existing jobs and up to 70% in construction, where people do not pay taxes and have no social protection. Informal workers account for more than half (54%) of the working-age population and most are young. The reasons for this workforce segment being so large include the low level of education of such workers, a complex and uncertain tax system, and a high labor tax burden on large businesses. Far from all job seekers are registered in the Public Employment Service centers. Low salaries push qualified workers to migrate abroad (e.g., to the Kazakhstan and the Russian Federation), but recent years' economic downturn outside the country has driven many migrants to return home and enter or reenter the domestic labor market. Lack of career guidance and labor market information and missing links between TVET and employers are exacerbating labor market problems.

The working-age population increased from 11 million in 1990 to almost 19 million in 2017, and an additional 4 million are expected to enter the labor force by 2030. The economy creates about 280,000 formal sector jobs per year on average (on a net basis) compared with the 600,000 annual entrants to the labor market. The economy needs to double the number of jobs created each year just to absorb new entrants. As a result, migration of workers to the Russian Federation and other CIS countries has been substantial. More than 2 million Uzbekistan citizens are estimated to reside abroad. Women's participation in the economy has continued to decline and informal employment to grow. Women's labor participation rate (33.1%) is far lower than the CIS average (50.2%).

The structure of domestic employment is moving gradually toward industry and services and away from primary sectors, especially agriculture. Services account for almost 80% of all new jobs. They require cognitive and noncognitive skills and attract graduates who follow education paths in appropriate fields. However, only 1.5% of the workforce is employed in high-tech industries and science. Males dominate high-paying jobs. Female workers in the labor market are mostly in professional and service occupations, and slightly fewer women than men are legislators, senior officials, and managers. Female participation in the labor force remains low.

Challenges include removing market distortions that undermine allocative efficiency and competition, eliminating regulatory barriers to business operations, promoting the reallocation of land to more productive uses, mitigating geographic inequities in access to social services, promoting the sustainable use and management of natural resources, making public administration more transparent and accountable, widening access to preprimary and tertiary education and improving the quality of the services, ensuring access to quality health care, and tackling the inefficiencies in social protection programs.

---

[67] This section is primarily based on K. Anderson, E. Ginting, and K. Taniguchi. 2020. *Uzbekistan—Quality Job Creation as a Cornerstone for Sustainable Economic Growth. Country Diagnostic Study*. Manila: ADB; World Bank. 2018. *Growth and Job Creation in Uzbekistan — An In-Depth Diagnostic*; and World Bank. 2020. *Uzbekistan Economic Outlook*.

[68] World Bank. Unemployment, Total (% of total labor force) (modeled ILO estimate) – Uzbekistan (accessed 1 November 2020).

Labor Migration

According to President Shavkat Mirziyoyev, 600,000–700,000 people enter the labor market every year. The economy can absorb 500,000 workers, meaning that up to 200,000 people might be compelled to take their chances abroad. The Russian Federation has historically been the main destination for expatriate laborers, although important if much smaller numbers find work in Kazakhstan, the Republic of Korea, Turkey, and the United Arab Emirates. According to official figures, about 2 million Uzbekistan nationals work outside the country, although the real number is likely far greater as many dispense with obtaining proper authorization, not least because of the expense entailed.[69]

Although most labor migrants have low-skilled jobs, thousands have completed advanced education and have high-skilled jobs. The government has launched a campaign to encourage the latter to return to their home country to reduce the shortage of highly skilled labor.

Regional Economic Cooperation and Labor Migration

Central Asia Regional Economic Cooperation. The Central Asia Regional Economic Cooperation (CAREC) Program is a partnership of 11 countries and development partners working together to promote development through cooperation, leading to accelerated economic growth and poverty reduction. "The program is a proactive facilitator of practical, results-based regional projects, and policy initiatives critical to sustainable economic growth and shared prosperity in the region. Since its inception in 2001 and as of 2019, CAREC has mobilized $38.6 billion in investments that have helped establish multimodal transportation networks, increased energy trade and security, facilitated free movement of people and freight, and laid the groundwork for economic corridor development."[70] According to ADB, one of the main sponsors of CAREC, the program "has recorded impressive achievements in regional economic cooperation, particularly in the areas of transport, energy, trade facilitation, and trade policy. From 2001 to end-September 2017, investments in member countries under CAREC have amounted to $30.5 billion, covering 182 projects" (footnote 70).

In October 2017, CAREC approved CAREC 2030, its strategy with the mission to be "a regional cooperation platform to connect people, policies, and projects for shared and sustainable development." The revised operational framework for CAREC 2030 groups activities into five clusters, including a new one on human development, which covers education and health.[71]

Within TVET, the point of departure for CAREC is the weakness experienced by most member countries. A recent ADB scoping study found that "key challenges include (i) the low quality of TVET programs; (ii) the skills gap, or mismatch between the skills provided on TVET programs and labor–market needs; and (iii) the absence or weakness of national qualifications systems. There is therefore a strong case for CAREC to consider strengthening the region's labor markets and making them more flexible. Potential areas for CAREC's support include harmonizing and strengthening the recognition of TVET qualifications across countries and strengthening labor market information systems (LMISs)" (footnote 70).

Regarding higher education, the CAREC scoping study is of the view that, by global comparison, standards remain low among countries in the region. "Higher education standards lack uniformity and have declined in several countries. In many, the quality of physical facilities and equipment has deteriorated, in large part due to low financing levels. This, in turn, makes it difficult for universities to attract high-quality faculty and students. Harmonizing degree systems and quality assurance offers an opportunity for CAREC to provide support" (footnote 70). The scoping study identified several areas for establishing regional cooperation in education and skills under CAREC.

---

[69] *Eurasianet*. 2020. Uzbekistan Pledges to Give Hopeful Migrant Laborers Loans. 19 August.
[70] CAREC. 2017. *CAREC 2030: Connecting the Region for Shared and Sustainable Development*. Manila.
[71] ADB. 2019. *Education and Skills Development under the CAREC Program. Scoping Study*. Manila.

III. Technical and Vocational Education and Training History, Policies, Systems, and Performance

A. Technical and Vocational Education and Training Policies and Systems in the Former Soviet Union

Our hypothesis is that an important key to understand TVET in the investigated countries is the legacy of the Soviet Union education system. During the Soviet period, science (research) was separated from education, and education from production and industry. A huge institution such as the Academy of Science coordinated all research, and the function of universities and institutes was limited to teaching. With few exceptions, the education system—and thus TVET—was homogenous across member states, except for the Baltic countries, which deviated from the general system on some minor points. During the many years of the Soviet era, the education system experienced several changes. All education institutions, including in TVET, were subordinated under the Ministry of Education for ideological reasons. For a few years, the Ministry of Education was called the Ministry of Higher, Secondary and Special Vocational Education. Science, education, and industry were coordinated through a single and centralized ministry, the State Planning Committee. This section focuses on the TVET landscape at the time of the collapse of the Soviet Union.

Since 1981, 10 years (11 in the Baltic republics) of secondary education were compulsory in the Soviet Union. Education was divided into 4 years of elementary school and 4 years of lower secondary education. After completing grade 8, students had the option of attending 2 years of upper secondary school, which prepared them to enter university, search for a job, or attend a technical training school.

In 1959, only 36% of the population had gone through secondary education; by 1986, that figure had grown to 70%. However, according to the 1989 census, three-fifths of people aged 15 years and older in what became the Russian Federation had completed secondary school and 8% had completed higher education. Wide variations in education attainment existed between urban and rural areas. The 1989 census indicated that two-thirds of the urban population aged 15 years and older had finished secondary school, compared with just under one-half of the rural population.

Technical and Vocational Education

Technical and vocational education in the Soviet Union was offered at two levels: lower and higher (Table 21). The title of a qualified worker in a specific vocation was associated with lower vocational education. A professional title was associated with higher vocational education.[72]

---

[72] This section is based on International Qualifications Assessment Service Government of Alberta. 2016. *International Education Guide*. Alberta, Canada.

Table 21: Technical and Vocational Education in the Soviet Union

Level of Vocational Education	Credential Name	Title on the Diploma	Number of Schools in 1989	Number of Students in 1989
Lower	Diploma of lower vocational education	Qualified worker (in a specific occupation)	5,900	2.5 million
Higher	Diploma of higher vocational education	Professional title (e.g., nurse, teacher)	4,500	4.2 million

Source: International Qualifications Assessment Service Government of Alberta. 2016. *International Education Guide*. Alberta, Canada.

Lower Vocational Education

Lower vocational programs were offered by professional technical schools (PTUs)[73] and secondary professional technical schools (SPTUs). The main distinction between them was that PTUs did not offer complete secondary education. Access to PTUs and SPTUs was usually obtained based on lower secondary education, but for a few occupations training was offered only after completion of upper secondary education. The length of the courses depended on the entry qualifications.

PTUs were developed after the World War II to train skilled workers in a wide variety of nonacademic professions, including carpentry, cookery, hairdressing, industrial and technical drawing, lathe operation, metalwork, machining, motor vehicle mechanics, plumbing, radio electronics, secretarial studies, sewing machine operation, and welding. PTUs offered narrow and applied instruction, about 80% of which was practical and 20% theoretical. Work experience was an integral part of all programs. Individuals who entered PTUs after lower secondary education followed different curricula than those who entered after upper secondary education.[74] Students without upper secondary education were offered some basic courses from the upper secondary curriculum.

SPTUs developed from PTUs in the 1970s, as many PTUs started to incorporate complete upper secondary education into their programs. Upper secondary education at SPTUs was fully equivalent to that at general secondary schools. Like PTUs, SPTUs offered vocational education in a wide range of trades. Programs incorporating upper secondary education usually lasted 3 years. Students took examinations in upper secondary subjects at the end of their second and third years. Exams were similar to those in general secondary schools. Only students who completed the full 3-year program obtained the equivalent of complete upper secondary education.

Creation of SPTUs was part of the effort to upgrade vocational training and increase to at least 50% the number of secondary school-leavers who transferred to SPTUs, while reducing the numbers in upper secondary schools to 40% or fewer. This was part of the overall policy of "acceleration of social and economic development," of modernization after the period of stagnation under Soviet leader Leonid Brezhnev. Creation of SPTUs was part of the recurring Soviet concern to prepare young people more effectively for working life, given that, in the 1980s, more than 60% of Soviet children were staying on in general school and working for qualifications entitling them to admission to higher education.[75]

---

[73] During the transformation to a market economy, PTUs suffered a huge blow as their graduates lost employment guarantees. Many PTUs were closed or merged and the number of students declined dramatically. Some PTUs were renamed and reformed into "lyceums" in an attempt to gain higher status and establish tuition fees.
[74] Some sources mention that for certain programs some PTUs did not conduct entrance examinations.
[75] A. Griffin and B. Bailey. 1994. Vocational Education in Russia in the Transition to a Market Economy. *The Vocational Aspect of Education*. 46 (2).

Higher Vocational Education

Institutions of higher vocational education in the Soviet Union were known as specialized secondary education institutions. They fell into three main categories: technicum (4-year technical school), *uchilishe* (higher technical college), and college (since 1989).

The technicum offered programs in technical and business fields and was the best structure in the system. Technicum graduates, did not receive a diploma of higher education but a diploma of professional technical specialist at the secondary level of education. The *uchilishe* offered programs for a range of skilled, nontechnical occupations, including preschool and primary school teaching and nursing. Some *uchilishe* were in higher education institutions. Colleges, which emerged in 1989, were created to educate highly trained specialists for the type of work previously entrusted to university-level graduates. As of 1990, 12 technicums were upgraded to colleges. Admission to a specialized secondary education institution was by entrance examination that tested knowledge of the lower secondary or upper secondary education curriculum, depending on the mode of entry. A college was the most competitive of all specialized secondary education institutions. Depending on the admission qualification, programs lasted 2–5 years. The typical duration was 2 or 3 years. To pursue higher education, technicum, *uchilishe or uchilishte,* and college graduates enrolled at universities and institutes, depending on their field of study.

In 1989, 67% of all higher vocational education students were enrolled in full-time programs, 7% in evening programs, and 27% in correspondence programs.

Students who successfully completed their course at a specialized secondary education institution were awarded diplomas of higher vocational education, including technician, nurse, or feldsher diplomas, among others.

Holders of a diploma of higher vocational education completed upper secondary education, either before or during their study at a specialized secondary education institution. Graduates of specialized secondary education institutions could continue their education at a higher education institution, but most entered the workforce.

Some colleges awarded the junior engineer diploma, which required an additional 1.5 years. College graduates with this credential could be granted advanced standing in the third year of appropriate higher education programs.

For both levels, the interaction between the employment system and the vocational education and training system was tightly integrated. The vocational schools were often effectively part of the human resource departments of large companies of which most were state-owned. Most of the practical training took place at the company, and the content of the training was typically developed in collaboration with the factory.[76] Jobs were secured for most graduates, demand for workers was insatiable, and employment was mostly for life.

The advantage of the model was the high level of labor market relevance of the training programs and, thus, secure employability of graduates. The limitation was the narrow specialization of the skills acquired by graduates, which limited their chances of finding a job at another company, not to mention in another field. The technological backwardness of many Soviet factories limited the possibility of trainees familiarizing themselves with state-of-the-art production techniques. At that time, students at vocational schools in the Central Asian republics could study at vocational schools in all republics, mainly in TVET institutions in the Russian Federation, Belarus, and Ukraine.

---

[76] The Soviet Union never established a public body with responsibility for national standards of qualifications. While courses were determined by the ministry, their implementation and the assessment of students were the responsibility of staff of the training institution.

Higher Education

Higher education was obtained at four categories of institutions: universities, institutes, *uchilishche*, and military schools and academies.

Only fully-fledged universities had the status of "university," of which there were only a few, mostly in the large regional centers. Institutes were specialized schools of higher education, mostly technical, which were usually subordinate to the ministry associated with their field of study. The largest were medical; pedagogical (for the training of schoolteachers); construction; and various transport (automotive and road, railroad, civil aviation) institutes. Some institutes were in every oblast capital while others were unique and only in big cities.

At the university level, degrees could be obtained in two phases: (i) the first was typically 5 years and resulted in the specialist diploma; and (ii) the second included two levels: candidate of sciences and doctor of sciences.

In 1991, there were 904 higher education institutions in the Soviet Union (Table 22). They enrolled 5.2 million full-time, part-time, or correspondence students. Higher education was administered by the State Committee for Public Education, while local committees were in charge of public education. In the case of some specialized institutions, corresponding ministries and departments assumed administrative responsibility jointly with the state committee.

Table 22: Number of Higher Education Institutions in the Soviet Union, 1991

Members of the Former Soviet Union	Number of HEIs	Percentage of all HEIs in the Soviet Union
Russian Federation	512	56.6%
Ukraine	147	16.3%
Armenia, Azerbaijan, Georgia, Kyrgyz Republic, Moldavia, Tajikistan, Turkmenistan	85	9.4%
Kazakhstan	55	6.1%
Uzbekistan	44	4.9%
Belarus	33	3.7%
Estonia, Latvia, Lithuania	28	3.0%
Total higher education institutions in the Soviet Union	*904*	*100.0%*

HEI = higher education institution.
Source: International Qualifications Assessment Service Government of Alberta. 2016. *International Education Guide*. Alberta.

The government encouraged students to go into pure and applied sciences, engineering, medicine, and agriculture. About 50% of all students majored in engineering, often with hopes of getting a prestigious, well-rewarded job in a large state institution. The best and the brightest were often picked for scientific jobs with military applications.

TVET Systems in the Former Soviet Union

After the collapse of the Soviet Union, central coordination ended. Countries started to build their education and TVET systems in a new format. Science and education were linked; universities began to engage actively in research. In most countries, the Ministry of Education was reorganized into the Ministry of Education and Science; in Tajikistan, even the Academy of Science became a structure of the ministry. Some countries implemented a new credit education system based on the European Union classification system for higher education, the so-called "Bologna Process." Some universities and TVET institutions were linked to specific economic ministries and enterprises. In the triangle of science, education, and industry, however, the connection between science and industry remains weak.

An element following the Soviet Union is the disjointed nature of the TVET system, with several ministries responsible for its different parts. In several countries such as Tajikistan, the Ministry of Education maintains an important role in regulating TVET, while the Ministry of Labor deals with the delivery of vocational training. The model has made it difficult to coordinate development of TVET and hampered collaboration with industry.

While the centralized TVET model practiced in the Soviet Union was instrumental in the rapid transformation of the member states from predominantly agricultural societies to economies with a strong manufacturing sector, the model's limitations became visible as manufacturing gradually became more sophisticated. In the long run, TVET lacked the flexibility to match the needs of a high-tech manufacturing and knowledge economy, with its required higher levels of specialization and technological change. The main challenges hampering modernization of TVET (and higher education) were

(i) extremely narrow areas of specialization, with early entry into TVET, creating rigid and inadaptable TVET;
(ii) centralized planning with little consideration of economic efficiency;
(iii) outdated curricula largely tied to a few industries; and
(iv) slow responsiveness to economic change.

Since the 1990s, the former Soviet Union and East European countries have adopted a wide range of reforms that relate to governance, quality, access, and relevance of TVET to achieve more flexible and more demand-responsive systems.

Reforms are classified into two major phases:
(i) Reforms initiated in the 1990s, focusing primarily on the governance and structure of education. Countries largely restructured the different sectors of education, including TVET, and donor organizations typically provided technical support in the process. Reforms reflected the countries' new legal frameworks and constitutions. The phase was marked by initial decentralization of regional and local service delivery. Delegating more responsibility to the management of the individual schools was a top priority.
(ii) The second phase, which is widely ongoing, focuses on modernizing TVET and higher education. Many countries have prepared policies specifically to adapt the structure of TVET delivery to the needs of the market economy. The reforms include the design of new curricula, design of national qualification frameworks, and development of systems for lifelong learning. Reforms are often accompanied by donor-funded investment in modern equipment and training materials.[77]

---

[77] C. Fawcett, G. El Sawi, and C. Allison. 2014. *TVET Models, Structure and Policy Reform. Evidence from the European and Eurasia Region.* Washington, DC: United States Agency for International Development.

B. Tajikistan

Technical and Vocational Education and Training Landscape

Primary education starts at age 7 and lasts 9 years: 4 years of primary and 5 years of basic (lower secondary) education. After graduating from basic education (grade 9), students may enroll in either general senior secondary education, secondary technical education, technical colleges, or IVET, provided by vocational lyceums. While general secondary education and IVET are completed with a grade 11 diploma, the secondary technical education diploma is equivalent to grade 12.

Initial Vocational Education and Training

IVET is provided by a network of 61 vocational lyceums[78] under the auspices of Ministry of Labor, Migration and Employment. The lyceums offer 1- and 2-year diploma courses to prepare students to continue their education in secondary and higher vocational institutions and, for those not eligible to do so, to prepare them for a decent job. The vocational lyceums provide training in 14 occupational areas: economics, technology, transport and equipment, electronic equipment, energy, chemical industry, light industry, mining, architecture and construction, agriculture, metallurgy, telecommunications, tourism and hotel services, consumer services, and public food. The occupational areas are divided into 96 working specialties. In addition to the regular diploma courses, almost entirely funded by the government, most lyceums offer short-term courses on a fee basis. The short-term courses primarily attract people such as returning migrant workers in need of a certificate acknowledging their practical competencies, e.g., as tractor or truck drivers. Students at the lyceums consist of those who have a government stipend and those who pay for themselves.[79] The tuition fee charged is nominal, which is why lyceums are attractive to many low-income household. Nearly 25% of students admitted into IVET do not complete the program.

The lyceums have a high level of autonomy on issues related to personnel (except for management). They enjoy the freedom to develop new training programs within their area of specialization, but these need approval by Ministry of Labor, Migration and Employment and/or the ministry within which they fall. IVET schools' autonomy is limited in the distribution of budgetary funds.[80]

Despite international support, most vocational lyceums face serious challenges, including dilapidated facilities and shortage of equipment and learning material. Because state-of-the-art equipment is lacking, most "practical" training is done by teachers using posters and the limited available outdated equipment. With few exceptions, the lyceums do not have facilities for students to conduct practical exercises by themselves. Many rural lyceums have dormitories for students and accommodation for teachers, but these are usually in serious need of rehabilitation and inappropriate for use.

About 10% of teachers undergo retraining every year, thanks mainly to international projects. For example, under ADB's Strengthening Technical and Vocational Education and Training Project in Tajikistan, from 2017 to 2020, more than 960 teachers were trained in the competency-based training (CBT) methodology (43.5% of the total number of teachers).

In 2018, 13,000 people graduated from IVET, of whom 30.3% were employed in various economic sectors, 26.5% decided to continue their studies at higher-level institutions, 39.2% looked for work, and another 4.0% joined the army.[81]

---

[78] Several lyceums are under ministries other than Ministry of Labor, Migration and Employment. Some specialize in academic subjects such as math, while one offers diplomas in music.
[79] In some countries, such short-term certified training is called recognition of prior learning.
[80] European Training Foundation. 2017: *Torino Process 2016–17. Tajikistan. Executive Summary*. Torino.
[81] Agency on Statistics under the President of the Republic of Tajikistan. 2019. *Labor Market in the Republic of Tajikistan*. Dushanbe. pp. 128–129.

Consultations with employers conducted under the ADB project revealed that more than 90% are not satisfied with the quality of training specialists in IVET.

Linkages between the lyceums and the local business community are essentially nonexistent. The managers interviewed did not see the importance of establishing such links and mentioned they would not know how to approach local businesses. However, there are three exceptions: one vocational lyceum specialized in training for the textile sector, one dealing with the aluminum industry, and a GIZ-sponsored lyceum in northern Tajikistan. ADB and the EU TVET projects discussed as follows are resolving this issue by involving employers in curriculum development and at the level of individual IVET schools.

Senior Secondary Technical and Vocational Education and Training

Senior secondary TVET is provided by 49 technical colleges (the total number of colleges is 72, including medical and teacher training colleges) managed by different ministries and SOEs, including the Ministry of Education and Science (20); Ministry of Culture (6); Ministry of Agriculture (2); Ministry of Health (15); Ministry of Energy (3); Ministry of Industry and Technology (1); Tajik Aluminum Plant (1); Hydropower Station of Rogun (1); and the Committee for Youth, Sports and Tourism (1). The technical colleges offer 3- and 4-year[82] courses intended to develop technicians, forepersons, and supervisors.

The government is actively improving the chain of institutions of secondary vocational education, where the creation of multidimensional education institutions is an important element. Thus, based on 11 secondary vocational education institutions, departments of primary vocational education have been created, which provide training in 16 professions. Being structural subdivisions of higher education institutions, nine colleges train midlevel specialists.

In addition to regular technical senior secondary programs, several technical colleges offer IVET programs and short-term training courses. For various reasons, including the fact that technical colleges are better equipped and enjoy better infrastructure than lyceums, and that secondary TVET is more prestigious than IVET, colleges have managed to attract a considerable number of so-called contract students, i.e., students who pay for themselves even though the tuition fee is substantial. As a result, colleges have more financial resources at their disposal than lyceums, although the government allocation per enrolled students is essentially the same for IVET and secondary TVET.

As for IVET, no tracer studies of secondary TVET graduates are available. However, those familiar with the TVET system think that most graduates opt for higher education and that not more than 20%–25% enter the labor market upon graduation. Ties to the private sector appear to be slightly more developed than for lyceums, but few technical colleges have formalized collaboration with private companies, except for internship arrangements.

Adult Learning Centers

In addition to IVET institutions, Ministry of Labor, Migration and Employment operates 35 adult learning centers (ALCs) offering short-term basic skills training and skills upgrading courses of up to 6 months. Some ALCs operate "satellites" catering to the training needs of local communities. The principal target groups are returning migrants, vulnerable youth, especially women, and, to a lesser extent, adults with limited literacy skills. In 2019, ALCs trained a total of 48,600 people, of whom 61.4% were women. ALCs also serve as centers for recognition of prior learning, i.e., accreditation of the undocumented skills of returning migrants. Except for a few that are donor supported, ALCs have dilapidated facilities, a shortage of learning materials, and poorly qualified instructors. Most ALC trainees are identified and funded through a voucher system by the employment agency under Ministry of Labor, Migration and

---

[82] The 4-year courses are for part-time students.

Employment, but a substantial number of trainees pay for the training themselves. With few exceptions, the entry requirement is completed secondary education.

Even though ALCs are primarily intended to provide underprivileged social groups with basic vocational skills to improve their economic conditions, severe underfunding means the centers are far from fulfilling this role, including as centers for certification of returning migrants. Certificates issued by ALCs have low recognition by employers because assessment equipment is inadequate and testing is not transparent.

Ministry of Labor, Migration and Employment operates several specialized resource centers dealing with issues of national significance, including the Engineering Pedagogical College in Dushanbe, which educates teaching staff for vocational lyceums in several engineering and agricultural occupations, and the Center for Training Methodology and Monitoring of Education Quality, which deals with monitoring, research, and curriculum development.

Higher Education

There are three types of higher education institutions: universities (*donishgoh*), academies (*akademiya*), and institutes (*donishkada*). Universities and academies offer bachelor, master, and specialist degrees, while institutes offer only bachelor and specialist degrees. In academic year 2016–2017, 39 higher education institutions were in operation, including the private Tajik State Pedagogical Institute in Panjakent and the University of Central Asia. The higher education institutions consist of 15 universities and 16 institutes with 7 branch campuses, and the National Conservatory. Several institutions have been established under the auspices of different authorities, including the armed forces.

The qualifications of teachers employed in higher education institutions have been gradually declining since the late 1990s. In 2011–2012, 26.7% of the 9,271 teachers had a doctoral or candidate of science degree as opposed to 35.0% in 2005–2006. Another source of concern is the high average age of faculty members. The older faculty members are the ones primarily holding higher qualifications, and their retirement over the next several years will drastically reduce the percentage of faculty having doctoral or equivalent qualifications.

Since 2004, the higher education system has undergone reforms to transfer it from the traditional Soviet education system to a European-inspired credit hour-based system. As in EU countries, the new system has three levels (bachelor, master, and doctoral), and while Tajikistan is not a signatory to the Bologna Declaration like the Kyrgyz Republic, it is compliant with the declaration.

School-to-Work Transition

Reflecting the government's effort to increase the population's education achievements, more than 80% have completed secondary education (grade 11) and above (Table 23). However, 70% of the labor force has no formal qualification apart from a general education certificate. About 20% of new entrants to the labor market have completed higher education. In comparison, youth who have completed either secondary VET at a college or IVET account for 13% of the total (2016). The percentage of the labor force with an IVET diploma has decreased, while the share of those with secondary TVET has increased. There are two reasons for this development: (i) the steadily increasing number of graduates from secondary TVET colleges relative to IVET, and (ii) private enterprises' preference for secondary TVET graduates over IVET graduates.

The numbers clearly illustrate the skewedness of the education system: too many young people start searching for jobs without any kind of labor market-relevant qualification, while a disproportionally high share continue to higher education.

Table 23: Profile of the Employed Population by Level of Completed Education, Labor Force Surveys, 2004, 2009, and 2016
(%)

	2004	2009	2016
Higher education	11.2	14.9	17.0
- Master	0.0	0.0	13.6
- Bachelor	0.0	0.0	3.4
Incomplete higher education	1.2	0.7	–
Secondary technical and vocational education and training (college)	7.9	6.3	8.9
Initial vocational education and training (lyceum)	7.5	7.9	3.9
Secondary general education	50.5	51.8	54.0
Basic general education (grade 9)	16.8	14.7	14.1
Elementary general education	4.2	2.9	2.1
Do not have elementary general education	0.7	0.7	0.0
Total	**100.0**	**100.0**	**100.0**

– = not available.
Source: TajStat. 2017. *Labor Force Survey 2016*. Dushanbe (accessed 28 October 2020).

The LFS-2016 recorded 155,758 officially unemployed people, which means that 6.9% of the total labor force was without a job that year. The unemployment rate among women was lower than among men (5.5% vs. 7.9%), probably because women are less likely than men to register as unemployed. In absolute terms, therefore, the number of women among those not in the labor force significantly exceeded the number of men, i.e., 1,806,249 women compared with 1,125,857 men. The unemployment rate for youth (aged 15–29 years) was 10.6%, double that of the group aged 30–75 years, and more than 1.5 times higher than the national average. The medium-term effect of COVID-19 on employment will be known only when the pandemic is fully under control, but preliminary estimates suggest that the effect will be visible for at least 12–18 months.

Unemployment among people with secondary education was 7.5%, and among those who did not have primary education was 2.5%. People with higher education had the highest unemployment rate (7.9%). Women with higher education found it more difficult to find a job than men. The unemployment rate recorded for IVET diploma holders was relatively low. A likely reason is that IVET diploma holders are more motivated to find a job in the informal sector than people with secondary and higher education.

There is no systematic career guidance for students in secondary school. There is only one Career Guidance Center in the country functioning under the Agency on Labor and Employment within Ministry of Labor, Migration and Employment. This center serves mainly the unemployed and, on its own initiative, sometimes conducts vocational guidance in schools. A total of 20,000–25,000 people (mostly job seekers) receive vocational guidance annually. There is no website for online career guidance. There is only a site for vacancies at the Agency of Labor and Employment (www.kor.tj), but it contains limited information.

Institutional Framework

Ministry of Education and Science is the principal ministry responsible for matters related to education, including early childhood and higher education. In March 2013, responsibility for IVET was transferred to Ministry of Labor,

Migration and Employment, with Ministry of Education and Science retaining responsibility over secondary TVET and licensing of IVET institutions and approval of IVET programs.

Ministry of Labor, Migration and Employment has three responsibilities. It oversees delivery of IVET and adult learning as well as provision of employment and migration services. Ministry of Labor, Migration and Employment's mandate includes policy development in these areas. All TVET-related certification is within the domain of Ministry of Education and Science, while IVET schools under Ministry of Labor, Migration and Employment are entitled to assess their students and trainees.

The Department for Migration Services under Ministry of Labor, Migration and Employment is mandated to establish up to 10 predeparture service centers for migrants in different parts of Tajikistan. So far, four centers have been established. While the one in Dushanbe is a full-fledged center, the three others are poorly staffed and lack basic equipment and facilities. The centers provide predeparture services to prospective migrants and assistance to returning migrants.

The division of responsibility between Ministry of Labor, Migration and Employment and Ministry of Education and Science has been a cause of debate and conflict ever since IVET was separated from technical secondary education and transferred to Ministry of Labor, Migration and Employment. Strong forces within the government argue that the separation was a mistake and that IVET should be shifted back to Ministry of Education and Science. However, there are no indications that this will take place.

Labor Market Monitoring

At present, demand and supply of labor is not systematically monitored at the TVET level. As a result, planning in the vocational education system at all levels is carried out without considering the real needs of the labor market. Existing legislation does not provide for the creation of an LMIS, but the draft law on training specialists based on labor market demand provides the basis for the creation of an LMIS, which will be managed by Ministry of Labor, Migration and Employment.

Tajikistan does not have regular skills assessment. The latest research was carried out in 2015 by an ILO project and in 2016 by an ADB project, both one-time studies. The draft law will provide the basis for introducing a mechanism to regularly assess skills needs.

Technical and Vocational Education and Training Management System

Many countries have integrated digital management information systems to manage their education and TVET systems. Typically, the management information system is used to keep track of students and their progress as well as of teaching staff and other key administrative data. Neither Ministry of Labor, Migration and Employment nor Ministry of Education and Science has such a database and information management system.

Technical and Vocational Education and Training Laws and Regulations

Today, TVET is a central element of the government's human resource development plans. The National Development Strategy (NDS) up to 2030 is based on three basic principles:[83] (i) prevention or prediction (reduction) of vulnerability in future development, (ii) industrialization or more efficient use of national resources, and (iii) innovation or development by integrating new developments into the social and economic mainstreams.

---

[83] Republic of Tajikistan. 2016. *National Development Strategy up to 2030*. Dushanbe.

The NDS 2030 emphasizes that "the main factor of this growth model can only be the human capital and its main core components—education and science—as the most important conditions of enhancing national security and encouraging national economic competitiveness. In this regard there is a need to be proactive and make a transition to a 12-year general education system and a large-scale implementation of international education standards in vocational training system" (footnote 83). The strategy emphasizes that the quality and scope of vocational education is important for economic competitiveness and that a close relationship must exist between the education system and the labor market to balance the supply of experts of different levels with labor market requirements.

The **Law on Education** is the basic law governing education, including IVET. The law regulates the structure and system of all levels of education, requirements for education institutions, education quality management, and public administration and control of the education system. The law establishes the basic principles, indicators, and requirements for the development, approval, and introduction of state education standards. Based on this law, separate decrees regulating the levels of vocational education, particularly initial vocational education, are adopted.

The **Law on Adult Education** (2017) provides the foundation for continuing professional development of human resources. The law provides for new concepts, such as lifelong learning; validation of occupational competencies and skills; occupational competency; and formal, nonformal, and informal education.

The **Law on Training of Specialists Taking into Account the Needs of the Labor Market** is the only law providing for the connection of VET with the labor market. The law imposes basic requirements for public policy in the field of training specialists in the vocational education system, considering the needs of the labor market, public–private partnership (PPP) in IVET, and the form of this partnership.

The **Law of 2003 on Promoting Employment** provides that the education system is oriented toward training the workforce in accordance with the needs of the labor market.

To resolve the unclear status of IVET and the overlapping mandates of Ministry of Labor, Migration and Employment and Ministry of Education and Science, the ADB project has drafted a **law on initial vocational education and training**. It provides for the creation of a vocational education system based on the needs of the labor market. The draft law envisages developing a national qualification framework (NQF) and competency standards based on the requirements of the NQF, delimiting powers of state bodies to manage IVET, engaging social partners in managing the system and employers in setting qualification requirements, assessing the quality of IVET institutions, and setting new standards of assessment of learning outcomes. The draft law was approved by the government on 28 September 2020 and has been submitted to the Parliament for endorsement.

Technical and Vocational Education and Training Reforms

In the years following Tajikistan's independence, TVET received little attention, either from the government or the international donor community. The devastating civil war further deteriorated the situation. The government adopted a "survival" strategy: existing facilities and teaching capacities were kept at a minimum operational level, and no resources were made available to improve capacities and adapt infrastructure to the realities of a changing society. As a result, TVET largely lost its immediate relevance for the employment system and its attractiveness for young people. The lower-level basic vocational schools developed a reputation for providing welfare for poor children rather than knowledge and skills relevant for work for young people.[84]

---

[84] European Training Foundation. 2006. *The Reform of Vocational Education and Training in the Republic of Tajikistan*. Torino.

Renewed interest in TVET came about in 2002 with the preparation of the Poverty Reduction Strategy. Although the strategy gave only marginal attention to TVET, at least the issues of the knowledge and skills of the workforce were put on the policy agenda. Today, TVET is a central element of the government's human resource development strategy.

During the last decade, international partners, especially ADB, the EU, and GIZ, have played an important role in modernizing TVET. Support includes policy advice, capacity building, development of occupational standards, update of curricula, development and production of learning material, and training of teachers and assessors. In addition to system support, the partners have financed selected equipment and material and, in the case of ADB, rehabilitation of several IVET institutions. Unlike ADB, the EU has no funds for rehabilitation. The need for support remains substantial.

ADB's first skills development project in Tajikistan was the Strengthening Technical and Vocational Education and Training Project, approved on 9 November 2015.[85] It supported initial and secondary TVET by introducing CBT, trained vocational teachers, upgraded facilities and equipment of vocational lyceums and colleges, and conducted a market-responsive and inclusive training survey.

Lessons learned from the project include the following: (i) quality short-term training is needed for out-of-school youth, (ii) employability and skills must be improved, (iii) labor market data collection and job classification systems should be strengthened, and (iv) more targeted support should be provided to tackle demand- and supply-side constraints for girls and women in the skills sector.[86]

The second major ADB support for TVET in Tajikistan is the Skills and Employability Enhancement Project, approved on 30 June 2020 (footnote 86). The project aims to promote inclusive growth through improving vocational, technical, and soft skills as well as employability of youth (aged 15–29 years), women, and labor migrants. It will support (i) construction of new migration service centers to provide comprehensive services to labor migrants, (ii) construction of model job centers to provide market-responsive training and employment services for youth and women, and (iii) capacity development of migration and employment agencies.

The National Education Development Strategy assumes a transition to CBT in VET, modularization of programs and adoption of an NQF (Box 1). Tajikistan has expressed its interest in aligning its education system to the principles of the Bologna Declaration. However, no decision has been made yet on the scope of the NQF or on the number of levels. Tajikistan is expected to apply an eight-level model given that it is the international norm and most Bologna members apply an eight-level qualification framework. The government's National Classification of Occupations (NCO) (2013) links occupations to qualifications. Four levels of qualifications are allocated in the NCO. It is not clear how the NCO will articulate with the future NQF.

Although the government officially subscribes to the CBT approach, it is uncertain that Ministry of Education and Science and Ministry of Labor, Migration and Employment understand it and how to roll it out. Communication between the two ministries is poor and their interpretation of CBT differs from that of the EU and ADB. The ADB

---

[85] ADB. 2015. *Report and Recommendation of the President to the Board of Directors: Proposed Loan, Grant, and Administration of Grant to the Republic of Tajikistan for the Strengthening Technical and Vocational Education and Training Project*. Manila. The memorandum of understanding of the project's midterm review mission in March 2019 stated that the project had been implemented successfully.
[86] ADB. 2020. *Report and Recommendation of the President to the Board of Directors Proposed Grant and Administration of Grant Republic of Tajikistan: Skills and Employability Enhancement Project*. Manila.

Box 1: Competency-Based Training

Competency-based training (CBT) is training and development that focuses on specific competencies or skills. What makes it unique is that the training programs are broken down into individual courses or modules. The modules focus on a single skill at a time, taking trainees through a course based on their mastery of each individual skill. Trainees must demonstrate their mastery of specific skills before moving on to further segments of training. Specific skills can be grouped into modules to emphasize specific types of training.

CBT is driven by five core principles:
(i) Focus on outcomes—what matters most is that the job is done to a degree that meets or exceeds an expected standard.
(ii) Greater workplace relevance—stronger focus on practical skills.
(iii) Outcomes as observable competencies—observing that a task has been done to meet or exceed a predetermined standard.
(iv) Use of assessments to judge competence—less focus on testing and more on whether a worker can or cannot perform a task to an expected standard in the work environment.
(v) Improvement of skills—more emphasis on improving skills performance rather than on just improving knowledge about the skills or task.

CBT has proved to be more effective than traditional teacher-centered training for two main reasons:
(i) It shifts the focus of the training from the trainer to the trainee. Classroom training runs on the trainer's schedule and at the trainer's pace. For many trainees, that pace is either too slow or too quick. Rather than teaching and lecturing in a traditional manner, in CBT the trainer becomes a mentor or a coach and guides learners as they try the skill and learn from their successes and failures. Many adult learners prefer this approach rather than listening to sage advice from the head of the class.
(ii) It aligns assessments and evaluations with competencies. Learners are assessed and evaluated against performance objectives and standards. When assessment results are low, or an evaluation is not successfully completed, practical exercises can be created to beef up the areas of skill that are lacking. The learner is told and shown what to do, how to do it, and to what standard. This gives the learner concrete goals that, when achieved, can be taken to work and demonstrated at the workplace.

Source: International Labour Organization. 2020. *Competency-Based Training (CBT): An Introductory Manual for Practitioners*. Geneva.

TVET project has launched a dialogue with Ministry of Labor, Migration and Employment on the issue, but no conclusion has yet been reached.

Following the uncertainty concerning the introduction of the NQF, the number of levels, and the definition of occupations, applying the ILO's International Standard Classification of Occupations (ISCO) has not been possible. Adoption of ISCO would improve the mobility of workers interested in searching for employment outside the country.

The EU and ADB both have a provision for strengthening the capacity of Ministry of Labor, Migration and Employment. So far, however, staff members have shown limited interest in taking advantage of this opportunity.

Finally, about 40 out of the more than 60 lyceums and a few ALCs will receive selected new equipment as part of ADB and EU assistance. With the support of ADB, the facilities of 21 lyceums will undergo various degrees of rehabilitation. Typically, because of resource constraints, rehabilitation has benefited only selected parts of the lyceums.

E-learning and Digital Skills

Information and communication technology (ICT) and digital skills are priorities in the NDS 2030. More than 10 higher education institutions are preparing ICT specialists, producing about 2,000 ICT graduates annually. Many TVET institutions offer basic ICT courses but few provide sophisticated programs dealing with digital technologies such as computer numerical control, robotics, web design, drones, and the Internet of Things.

Tajikistan lags behind other countries in the region in e-governance and the use of ICT in public administration. In 2018, Tajikistan ranked 131 in the e-government development index (0.422), 9 points lower than in 2012.[87] Even the system of the Agency of Labor and Employment does not have a unified information network. Although many ministries, departments, and education institutions have their own websites, they are often not updated, serve mainly as a business card, and do not exchange information with the public and students. The websites are not used for effective management. The introduction of ICT into higher and secondary vocational education will help develop more flexible learning and improve the efficiency and quality of education. The development of ICT can help solve communication problems, which is a priority of the NDS 2030. Training can be made available online anywhere in the country, provided that a network of inexpensive and fast internet connection is developed and appropriate resources and software products are created. Lessons and videos can be offered through the internet, expanding the boundaries of formal standardized education. Activities in this direction could become a priority of education, especially because many education products are already developed and used all over the world and can be adapted to local conditions.

The government has approved The Concept Paper on Digital Economics in the Republic of Tajikistan (Decree 642, 30 December 2020), which covers the period up to 2040.

Technical and Vocational Education and Training Response to COVID-19

In April 2020, Ministry of Labor, Migration and Employment adopted a crisis plan for the impact of COVID-19 on the labor market. The plan includes 12 measures of social support for vulnerable groups but does not provide for any measures to develop distance learning.

The education system had serious challenges in switching to online education. For distance learning, the level of training and the availability of the internet proved to be a serious constraint. Schoolchildren and students in rural regions were not able to study using internet resources because of the lack of internet coverage in distant and mountainous areas. Because of the prohibitive cost and low speed of the internet, studying online will become an additional financial burden that many cannot afford. The only available solution was to announce school vacation and transition to independent study.

Ministry of Education and Science is developing measures to organize online training in secondary schools and in higher education institutions but not in primary and secondary professional education (IVET and secondary TVET).

With the improvement of the situation since August 2020, education in all institutions resumed in accordance with Ministry of Education and Science rules to prevent COVID-19. The measures include the use of masks, hand washing and disinfection, disinfection of schoolyards and classrooms, appointment of doctors on duty at the entrances of education institutions, daily body temperature measurements, social distancing, and urgently taking care of individuals with symptoms of illness.[88]

---

[87] United Nations: E-government Development Index. 2020. www.un.org/development/desa/publications/publication/2020-united-nations-e-government-survey

[88] This section was provided by Ministry of Labor, Migration and Employment.

C. Other Central Asian Countries

As in Tajikistan, education systems have undergone considerable reforms in other Central Asian countries. Today, the countries have similar education systems, with the following levels:[89]
(i)   preschool education (2–3 years);
(ii)   general primary and lower secondary education (9 years);
(iii)   general vocational and technical upper secondary education (2–4 years);
(iv)   tertiary education—bachelor degree or postsecondary professional diplomas (3–4 years); and
(v)   postgraduate education—specialist diploma, candidate of science, master and doctoral degrees (1–5 years).

TVET systems have developed differently. In Kazakhstan, the Kyrgyz Republic, and Turkmenistan, as in Tajikistan, there are two levels of TVET: IVET and upper secondary TVET.

Typically, secondary TVET education is provided through a network of schools, some attached to higher education institutions:
(i)   **PTU.** Graduates receive a junior specialist diploma equal to a certificate of complete secondary education.
(ii)   **Technicum.** Graduates receive a junior specialist diploma equal to a certificate of complete secondary education.
(iii)   **Lyceum or various training courses offered by higher education institutions or industry.** Graduates receive a junior specialist diploma or diploma of academic lyceum equal to a certificate of complete secondary education.

Across all the countries, the linkages between different levels of the education system are mainly linear and confined to formal testing, while TVET policies continue to focus on youth and first-time learners (aged 16–24 years). The quality of adult education has been largely neglected, even though these countries have had active labor market measures and training initiatives for the unemployed in place for several years.[90]

Kazakhstan

Recently, Kazakhstan has been extending its schooling system from 11 to 12 years in selected schools. This extension was scheduled to be implemented nationwide from 2020. However, only a small number of "experimental" schools offer a 12-year curriculum (5+5+2), such as the Nazarbayev Intellectual Schools, a network of 20 schools targeting "gifted" pupils where admission is extremely competitive. There is at least one such school per region. In contrast, poorly resourced small-class schools, which dominate in rural areas, account for about 11% of the total student population (footnote 90).

As part of the drive to a stronger market orientation of the economy, the government has launched a series of initiatives to modernize the education and training system (footnote 90). In 2010, Kazakhstan was the only Central Asian country to sign the Bologna Declaration. As a result, a three-level model was introduced based on a credit system reflecting acquired knowledge. Full transition to a new structure took place in 2010. From January 2019, Kazakhstan transferred to a new credit system, fully compatible with the European Credit Transfer and Accumulation System.

---

[89] United Nations Educational, Scientific and Cultural Organization (UNESCO). 2020. *Ensuring Lifelong Learning for all in Kazakhstan, Kyrgyzstan, Tajikistan and Uzbekistan.* Paris.

[90] Progress has drawn heavily on international support, especially from the World Bank. It is now working with national authorities and actors on the – Kazakhstan Skills and Jobs Project 20162020. Also see World Bank. 2021. Kazakhstan Skills and Jobs Project. https://projects.worldbank.org/en/projects-operations/project-detail/P150183.

In 2012, Kazakhstan adopted an NQF based on the Bologna Declaration:
(i) bachelor program—at least 4 years (depending on the field of study),
(ii) master program—1 year (professional) or 2 years (scientific), and
(iii) doctoral program—3 years.

Legislative changes made in 2014 and the adoption of NQFs in 2012 led to TVET reforms, including the adoption of a dual approach (work-based learning) and the development of professional standards. While the dual approach provided broader opportunities for enterprise-based training, it reached only 10% of TVET students. The government established the National Council for Vocational Education and regional and sectoral councils to work with businesses and industries on plans to train personnel, forecast the need for specialists, and develop professional standards. To involve employers in defining TVET content and skills, the government assigned the National Chamber of Entrepreneurs the mandate to approve occupational standards and gave it a leading role in developing occupational standards via sector associations, except for a few public sector occupations. More than 100 new occupational standard–based curricula have been developed. The government has taken actions to develop public–private dialogue and involve employers in TVET. For instance, the National Chamber of Entrepreneurs has established a network of assessment centers to certify graduates and started training and registering occupational standard experts. Institutional capacity to forecast the needs for skills and gather labor market information has improved. The Center for Workforce Development in the Ministry of Labor and Social Protection of the Population conducts short- and medium-term analysis and plans to develop a skills-forecasting road map. The reforms have drawn heavily on international support, especially from the World Bank KZ Skills and Jobs Project 2016–2020.[91]

The government has taken several initiatives to increase transition to higher education. Because of low scores in national exams for higher education, many vocational college graduates are unable to continue to a higher education institution. Therefore, in 2016 Ministry of Education and Science amended the admission rules, which simplified the transition to higher education. The amendments allow TVET graduates to retake the Comprehensive Test, creating flexible pathways between different levels and sectors of the education system and promoting lifelong learning. More efforts are being made to increase the prestige of TVET and to attract more students to colleges. For instance, in 2014, Kazakhstan entered the World Skills International Competition and held its first national championship.

A growing number of evening schools offer second-chance equivalency education for young people who left school without completing secondary education and more and more nonformal training programs. However, there is no official system to certify and recognize nonformal and informal learning, which is believed to be an obstacle to young people and adults participating in nonformal education.

In 2018, the total student population was about 500,000, with females comprising 54.3%. About 14,000 international students are enrolled in higher education institutions (Table 24).

Despite the government's effort to better align its vocational education, training, and higher education systems to labor market demand, the system still faces several challenges, according to the World Bank. First, TVET lacks the legal and quality assurance frameworks needed to incentivize systemic change. "Not surprisingly, employer surveys continue to point to the need to improve training program offerings to grow the workforce skills needed in a diversified and modern economy. In higher education, there is a need to continue encouraging partnership agreements between higher education providers, employers, and industry-based innovation research. Finally, the agendas of early childhood development and lifelong learning are still nascent

---

[91] OECD. 2017. *Kazakhstan: Monitoring Skills Development through Occupational Standards*. Paris.

Table 24: Key Features of Education in Kazakhstan

Literacy level (population over 15 years old) in 2018	99.8%
Gross enrollment rate, grades 10–11 (academic lyceums)	NA
Gross enrollment rate, vocational upper secondary education	41% (2015)
Gross enrollment tertiary education (2019)	62%
Number of technical colleges (2019–2020)	740
Number of students at technical colleges (2019)	475,443
Number of higher education institutions—state-owned (2019)	55
Number of higher education institutions—private or corporatized (2019)	70
Number of students at higher education institutions (2019)	604,300
Students in upper secondary education enrolled in vocational programs	40% (2016)

NA = not available.
Source: United Nations Educational, Scientific and Cultural Organization. 2020. *Kazakhstan*. Paris; World Bank DataBank (accessed 29 October 2020). and KazStat (Ministry of National Economy). 2020. *Education Statistics*. Astana.

in the country. Working-age adults have limited opportunities to re-skill or upskill, whether on the job, in the workplace facilities, or in a network of accredited training providers that provide access to and high-quality short-term training opportunities."[92]

Another concern is that "employment growth has been higher for occupations that require medium to high skills, although many workers remain low-skilled. In line with changes in the economy, manual workers, operators, and skilled agricultural workers have been in less demand in the last decade compared to high and medium-skilled workers in other sectors. For instance, between 2003 and 2013, demand for workers with high qualifications increased by 5.8%, while demand for manual laborers increased only by 1.6% and demand for skilled agricultural workers decreased by 3.6%. Despite growth in high and medium skill employment, a large share (approximately one-fifth) of workers remains low-skilled and work in manual jobs" (footnote 92).

Last, although demand orientation of TVET is high on the government's agenda, no systematic assessment of skills needs and gaps in the labor market is conducted and tracer studies are conducted only occasionally.

Kyrgyz Republic

The education system has five levels. Pre-school education covers children up to 6 years old. Compulsory primary education covers grades 1–4 (usually aged 7–10 years) and lower secondary education grades 5–9 (11–15 years). Upper secondary school lasts 2 years is not compulsory and can be completed in general education, vocational, or specialized technical schools. Postsecondary schooling is available through vocational schools and specialized technical schools, and universities. Education is overwhelmingly provided by the public sector, which enrolled about 98% of all preprimary (up to 6 years) and general secondary (grades 1–11) students in 2016.

However, since gaining independence, the country has faced significant challenges in meeting its citizens' education needs. Almost 30 years later, the cumulative effects of insufficient financing, aging or inadequate materials, dilapidated infrastructure, and limited professional capacity among teachers still result in poor literacy among youth. In 2014, only 35% of children in grade 4 were reading at their grade level.

---

[92] World Bank. 2019. *Country Partnership Framework 2020–2025*. Washington, DC.

Table 25: Key Features of Education in the Kyrgyz Republic

Literacy level (population over 15 years old) in 2018	99.6%
Gross enrollment rate, grades 10–11 (academic lyceums)	53.4%
Gross enrollment rate, vocational upper secondary education (2014)	37%
Gross enrollment, tertiary education (2019)	42.3%
Number of higher education institutions—state-owned (2017–2018)	31
Number of higher education institutions—private and corporatized (2017–2018)	24
Students in upper secondary education enrolled in vocational programs (2015)	35%

Source: United Nations Educational, Scientific and Cultural Organization. 2020. http://uis.unesco.org/en/country/kyz. Paris; World Bank DataBank (accessed 3 November 2020).

While enrollment rates for grades 1–9 are near universal (above 99% for grades 1–4 and 98% for grades 5–9), with no disparity between girls and boys, enrollment drops off at upper secondary school. Net attendance rates for grades 10–11 were estimated to be 79% for boys and 86% for girls in 2014 (Table 25).[93]

Vocational education is offered through three kinds of courses: (i) a 3-year course mixing vocational and general education and preparing for higher education, (ii) a 2-year course mixing vocational and general education (without preparation to higher education), and (iii) a 10-month course of pure vocational education (also open to adults). Vocational education is given in professional lyceums and vocational technical colleges. About one-third of colleges providing secondary TVET are affiliated with higher education institutions. When entering higher education, graduates of these colleges are given credit for their previous education.

A recent national study indicates (i) TVET participation rates are remarkably low (just 10.6% of youth aged 15–24 years are in TVET, 2.3% in primary TVET, and 8.3% in secondary TVET); (ii) a large proportion of youth (27.9%) are NEET, and in some regions this proportion exceeds 30%; (iii) among school graduates (grades 9–11), 27.9% enroll in TVET, while 21.0% enter higher education and more than 51% enter the labor market or join the pool of those who are NEET and lack any skills training. The skills profile of TVET graduates does not correspond to regional economic priorities.

Only a fraction of the many skilled occupations (434) and specializations (243) are taught; the lack of diversity in training programs makes TVET less attractive and skews the gender distribution, with mostly male TVET students in lyceums and female TVET students in colleges. While secondary TVET college enrollment has increased significantly, teaching in colleges remains highly theoretical and does not adequately equip youth with the practical skills they need in the labor market. Many new teachers lack preservice training, and in-service training opportunities for existing teachers are limited. These weaknesses are reinforced by a shortage of sophisticated training materials and equipment.[94]

There have been several attempts to reform the TVET system, mainly focusing on IVET, including the shift to learning outcomes and employer and private sector involvement. In 2017, Ministry of Education and Science launched a project supported by ADB, which envisaged the possibility of integrating initial and secondary vocational education and "establishing educational trajectories for vocational education" to ensure continuity and progression pathways of initial and secondary vocational education.[95]

---

[93] World Bank. 2019. *Project Information Document—Education*. Washington, DC.
[94] ADB. 2017. *Proposed Grants Kyrgyz Republic: Skills for Inclusive Growth Sector Development Program*. Manila.
[95] UNESCO. 2020. *Ensuring Lifelong Learning for all in Kazakhstan, Kyrgyzstan, Tajikistan, and Uzbekistan*. Paris.

Higher education is provided by universities, academies, institutes, and specialized higher education institutions (conservatories, higher military education institutions, and others). Bachelor and master programs are available in a wide range of specializations such as physics and math, ICT, natural sciences, human sciences, social sciences, pedagogical education, health care, culture and art, economics and management, service sector, agriculture, energy, transport technology, and electronics.

Although the government has launched reform of higher education, education standards and professional standards have been criticized for not responding to labor market needs. Outdated curricula combined with obsolete equipment and shortage of qualified teaching staff are some of the challenges faced by most higher education institutions.[96]

Although cooperation between higher education institutions and employers is not officially regulated, it is a part of the practice of most institutions. Production practice is a compulsory element of most first-cycle education programs. Usually, employers are invited to participate in the work of the state attestation commissions during the final certification of students. Several universities have bilateral agreements on training, practice, and internship of students.

Like Kazakhstan, the Kyrgyz Republic has developed and adopted an NQF. All qualifications—TVET, general, and higher education—are included in the NQF. Some levels match the Russian Federation qualification system, which is supposed to ease recognition of qualification levels for the external labor market. Despite its adoption, the NQF is not yet fully operational. However, it is perceived as having an impact on the quality of education and serving as an important mechanism to ensure flexible pathways between education levels, even though more solid evidence must be gathered (footnote 96).

In 2018, the concept of e-learning and digital management was developed and approved by Ministry of Education and Science and is under consideration by an interministerial working group.

Turkmenistan

Turkmenistan is one of the Central Asian countries with the least information on the education system's performance.

Since the dissolution of the Soviet Union, Turkmenistan has implemented significant changes to its education system. Beginning in 1991, the country's first president introduced an education policy requiring only 9 years of schooling. The second president, who took office in 2006, established new standards of accountability in many aspects of his new education policy, the most notable being attempts to follow international norms relating to education and children's rights.

In 2013, a new education system required a standard 12 years of schooling for all children but retained many features of the structural framework of Soviet-era education. The system is undergoing reforms to produce highly skilled citizens so that the country can participate in international activities or undertakings. The reforms include educating citizens who can write the country's new history. The government is restructuring the primary and secondary school system to Western standards, which have shorter curricula but more vocational training and human resource development.[97]

---

[96] European Commission. 2017. *Overview of the Higher Education System—Kyrgyzstan*. Bonn.
[97] K. Schrag. 2017. Education in Turkmenistan. *Borgen Magazine*. 15 November.

Today, Turkmenistan has a 3-4-6-2 formal education structure. Three years of preprimary school are followed by four years of primary school. Secondary education is divided into two cycles: lower secondary and general upper secondary. Lower secondary—general basic education (first stage)—consists of grades 5–10; upper secondary—general basic education (second stage)—consists of grades 11–12 and culminates in a certificate of general secondary education.[98]

School-leavers graduate at 18 and can proceed either to higher education, higher professional education, secondary VET,[99] or IVET, or they may look for a job. The new regulations have been applied since 2013/14. The first students who have completed the compulsory cycle of 12 years' basic education will graduate in 2020.

Basic education is provided by state education institutions and is free of charge and obligatory. Secondary VET, IVET, and higher education are provided by state and non-state education institutions. While secondary VET and IVET are mostly paid for, higher education is free of charge, except for the International University for Humanities and Development and the Oguz Khan University of Engineering Technologies.

Initial VET[100] is concerned with training semi-qualified workers in all areas of economic activity following the completion of general secondary education. IVET is provided in various types of schools, including secondary VET schools, specialized lyceums, and higher education institutions that hold the relevant licenses. IVET is provided on a full-time and part-time (evening classes) basis for 3–18 months. IVET is widely sought by youth who did not make it to secondary VET or higher education.

There are 128 accredited vocational schools and training centers offering vocational training courses, of which 65 are subordinated to corresponding sectoral ministries and departments. As a rule, IVET courses are not subject to government funding. Enrollment in IVET courses has shown a clearly decreasing trend since 2012 (Table 26). The annual intake in IVET courses is almost three times higher than total enrollment, reflecting the short duration of most of the courses.

No information is available regarding the employability of IVET graduates, i.e., in the form of tracer studies.

According to the Ministry of Education, there are 268 specialties at the IVET level. Most training courses are provided in popular fields of study, such as accountancy, bookkeeping, and office work, but there are also specialized training courses in agriculture, textiles, construction, energy, and economics.

Table 26: Initial Vocational Education and Training in Turkmenistan (Vocational Schools)

	2012	2013	2014	2015	2016	2017
No. of IVET accredited schools	130	131	131	130	129	128
No. of students (enrollment)	51,800	49,200	37,400	34,100	35,500	36,700
Intake of new students	120,600	118,500	92,700	87,700	83,200	90,400
No. of graduates	119,900	118,700	101,800	88,300	79,400	86,500

IVET = initial vocational education and training, no. = number.
Source: State Committee on Statistics of Turkmenistan. 2018. *Statistical Yearbook of Turkmenistan*. Ashgabat.

---

[98] Education is not separated into different levels. Rather, it is one continuous process.
[99] "Secondary VET" might be misleading, as enrollment in schools offering the program requires successful completion of secondary education.
[100] Initial VET is sometimes referred to as "primary vocational education."

Secondary VET is concerned with training qualified workers and technicians. It is provided in various types of secondary schools (including colleges and secondary professional schools) and in higher education institutions that hold the relevant licenses. Training is provided on a full-time basis. The courses vary from 24 to 36 months. In 2017, 42 institutions provided secondary VET with a total enrollment of 21,600, which is almost twice as many enrolled in 2012 (Table 27). According to one source, 36 of secondary VET schools are affiliated to ministries related to their line of specialization.

Women account for 55% and men 45% of those in secondary VET. Women predominate in education, health care, economics, tourism, and culture and art.

Secondary VET is completed either with a diploma in general or vocational subjects or a vocational education diploma. However, graduates do not receive their diplomas before they have completed 2 years of mandatory service for the state. For men, the 2 years are typically spent in the armed forces.

As in other Central Asian countries, VET in Turkmenistan is provided in narrowly defined professional profiles and in only a few cases do students also learn general education disciplines or other subjects. This leaves graduates with considerably less opportunity for continuing their education at higher education institutions.[101] Not much is known about the labor market absorption of secondary VET graduates or employer satisfaction with their competencies and skills.

Several training and curriculum improvement activities are being implemented in collaboration with foreign companies. For example, General Electric (United States) has established a training center in Ashgabat, equipped with advanced technologies and connected via telecommunication systems with large construction sites and power plants. The center provides training for specialists and the teaching staff and students at engineering higher education institutes. The Hyundai Engineering Company (Republic of Korea) has opened a center to train specialists for the oil and gas industry. The capacity of the center is 400 people per year. STORM Training Center in cooperation with ES Hazar Doganlary and Caspian Driller (Singapore) has organized distance learning and e-learning courses to train specialists to use the STORM platform (Russian Federation).[102]

As with IVET, no information is available on labor market absorption of graduates from secondary VET schools or the share that opts for higher education.

Table 27: Secondary Vocational Education and Training in Turkmenistan (Secondary Professional Schools)

	2012	2013	2014	2015	2016	2017
No. of sec. prof. schools	32	37	40	42	42	42
No. of students (enrollment)	11,600	14,500	17,200	20,000	21,500	21,600
Intake of new students	5,800	6,600	7,800	8,400	8,500	8,300
No. of graduates	2,500	3,600	4,900	5,44	7,000	8,000

no. = number, sec. prof. = secondary professional
Source: State Committee on Statistics of Turkmenistan. 2018. *Statistical Yearbook of Turkmenistan*. Ashgabat.

---

[101] While up to 80% of the curriculum consists of trade-related theoretical subjects, students have two intervals of internships in predominantly state-owned enterprises.
[102] European Commission and the Education, Audiovisual and Culture Executive Agency. 2017. *Overview of the Higher Education System, Turkmenistan*. Brussels. p. 4.

Continuing education. Several state education institutions provide adult education in foreign languages, management, marketing, economics, and computer literacy. Of the total number of registered education institutions, about 30% are engaged in adult education. Skills upgrading courses are normally fee-based.

According to official statistics, a total of 5,800 employees were trained, retrained, and trained in a second profession in 2017. However, some of the training activities recorded under IVET were skills upgrading of the existing labor force.

Higher education institutions comprise 6 universities, 17 institutes, 1 academy, and 1 conservatory (Table 28). Several new higher education institutions have been opened since 2015, including the Turkmen Agricultural Institute, the Naval Institute, the Institute of International Relations of the Ministry of Foreign Affairs, the Turkmen State Institute of Finance, the Turkmen State Institute of Oil and Gas, the Architecture and Construction Institute (Polytechnic), and the Institute of National Security and Frontier Institute (Military Academy).

The higher education programs are for 4–7 years, depending on the specialization. Few higher education institutions offer master and doctoral programs. More than two-thirds of the students enrolled in higher education programs are in midlevel (bachelor) programs.[103] In 2018, Turkmenistan launched the process of aligning the education system to Bologna standards by introducing diplomas at the bachelor, master, and doctoral levels and several specialist diplomas.

All higher education institutions are state owned, subordinated to corresponding sectorial ministries, and most are financed from the state budget. As most universities cannot enroll fee-paying students, the total number of places is highly limited, causing fierce competition. The quotas for higher education are determined based on applications from sectoral ministries and departments classified by specialty and region. Based on this, the Ministry of Education develops an integrated plan of admission.

Access to higher education and postsecondary TVET is based on entrance exams. There are no pathways within the education system, i.e., there is no preferential access to specific disciplines for students who have completed specific courses during their previous education or studies. Students must pass three entrance exams and the most successful are admitted on a competitive basis. Some sources indicate that personal connections often play a role in gaining entry and later advancement.

Table 28: Higher Education in Turkmenistan (Universities and Institutes)

	2012–2013	2013–2014	2014–2015	2015–2016	2016–2017	2017–2018
No. of higher educ. institutions	23	24	24	24	25	25
Students admitted	6,700	7,000	8,000	8,300	8,500	9,400
No. of students (enrollment)	27,400	29,800	32,600	35,500	38,000	41,200
No. of graduates	4,400	4,900	5,200	5,900	6,000	

educ. = education, no. number.
Source: State Committee on Statistics of Turkmenistan. 2018. *Statistical Yearbook of Turkmenistan*. Ashgabat.

---

[103] Turkmenistan has only recently introduced the Bologna model; therefore, the statistics do not distinguish between bachelor and master students.

According to information from the Ministry of Education, there are about four times more applicants than places available at higher education institutions. In 2017–2018, 30% more students were admitted to higher education institutions than in 2012–2013. However, there remains a gender gap for those studying in higher education institutions: 34% of students are women and 66% men.

After graduating from a higher education institution (5 years), specialists are assigned to workplaces, where they are obliged to work for 2 years. Then they receive a university diploma. Graduates admitted to the university according to regional quotas are obliged to work in the regions they come from.

Uzbekistan

Uzbekistan is the only country in the region that offers 11 years of compulsory education; in the other four countries, 9 years of education are compulsory as in many European countries (Table 29). In 1998–2017, Uzbekistan offered 12 years of compulsory school education. From 2017, however, the country changed back to 11 years as the reform disappointed and troubled parents and children. Given that Uzbekistan offers 11 years of compulsory education, after grade 9 students progress either to general upper secondary education or to VET. Most (93%) are directed toward TVET at a professional college, where the students in grades 10 and 11 have 1 day per week of vocational education, where they focus on a specific profession in a college attached to that industry. The fewer students who aim to enter university usually move to an academic lyceum for grades 10 and 11 (footnote 95). All students in TVET are funded by the state as part of the compulsory education system.

After grade 11, students have the opportunity to attend professional or vocational colleges (postsecondary TVET level or tertiary education) corresponding to different qualifications.

Non-university-level tertiary vocational education is provided by national enterprise training centers and several business schools, as well as lyceums that train professionals in new economics and service fields.

During the last 5 years, the government has invested heavily in building new colleges and lyceums and improving existing ones. Consequently, the number of upper secondary students has more than doubled.[104] The government plans to organize in each region one exemplary professional school, college, and technical school.[105]

Table 29: Key Features of Education in Uzbekistan

Literacy level (population over 15 years old) in 2016	100%
Gross enrollment rate grades 10–11 (academic lyceums)	10%
Gross enrollment rate vocational upper secondary education	90% (2018)
Gross enrollment tertiary education (2019)	12.6%
Number of higher education institutions (2019–2020)	119
Students in upper secondary education enrolled in vocational programs	93% (2016)

Source: United Nations Educational, Scientific and Cultural Organization. 2020. *Uzbekistan.* Paris; and World Bank DataBank (accessed 20 October 2020).

---

[104] K. Anderson, E. Ginting, and K. Taniguchi. 2020. *Uzbekistan—Quality Job Creation as a Cornerstone for Sustainable Economic Growth.* ADB. Manila.
[105] *UZ Daily.* 2020. New Opportunities in the Education System of Uzbekistan Discussed. 30 April.

However, to cope with the increasing number of secondary education graduates, the government has reduced the number of academic lyceums and professional colleges (Tables 30 and 31) while increasing the number of higher education institutions (Table 32).

Acknowledging that improving the content and quality of TVET is important, the government has embarked on a reform of the TVET system to ensure that it is relevant to the labor market's needs. National stakeholders are developing a new vision for TVET. Consequently, new institutional arrangements, governance, and organization of TVET institutions are emerging. The government plans further consultations with key national stakeholders to come to an agreement on the overall architecture of TVET systems, their governance and funding, qualifications and quality assurance, and links with the labor market, particularly the roles of the private sector and industries in TVET.

Table 30: Number of Academic Lyceums and People Enrolled in Uzbekistan

Academic Year	Number of Academic Lyceums	Total Students	Female	Male
2015–2016	144	103,671	45,287	58,384
2016–2017	144	101,339	44,698	56,641
2017–2018	123	85,798	37,251	48,547
2018–2019	123	71,809	29,502	42,307
2019–2020	92	43,193	15,679	27,514

Source: StatUz. 2020. *Statistical Yearbook Uzbekistan*. Tashkent.

Table 31: Number of Professional Colleges and People Enrolled in Uzbekistan

Academic Year	Number of Professional Colleges	Total Students	Female	Male
2015–2016	1,423	1,394,903	685,055	709,848
2016–2017	1,422	1,358,064	665,562	692,502
2017–2018	1,433	1,077,364	523,324	554,040
2018–2019	1,414	656,297	327,432	328,865
2019–2020	1,025	239,239	129,024	110,215

Source: StatUz. 2020. *Statistical Yearbook Uzbekistan*. Tashkent.

Table 32: Number of Higher Education Institutions and People Enrolled in Uzbekistan

Academic Year	Number of HEIs	Total Students	Female	Male
2015–2016	69	264,291	163,434	100,857
2016–2017	70	268,281	165,824	102,457
2017–2018	72	297,689	178,509	119,180
2018–2019	98	360,204	200,805	159,399
2019–2020	119	440,991	238,454	202,537

HEI = higher education institution.
Source: StatUz. 2020. *Statistical Yearbook Uzbekistan*. Tashkent.

Guided by coordination councils from regional and national professional colleges, the system benefited from the participation of employers' associations and trade unions in policy making to ensure that it tackles issues of graduates' labor market entry. Although the progress of developing the vocational and technical education system has been impressive, specifically in infrastructure development and coverage, its quality and governance need improving. A survey of more than 200 enterprises in Uzbekistan indicates that, while 80% of firms are satisfied with the skills of university graduates, less than 60% express satisfaction with the skills of TVET graduates (footnote 105).

Higher education is undergoing significant reforms. Starting in 2017, the focus has been on quality graduate training by the upgrading of academic staff qualifications, development of international relations, opening of new institutions, establishment of joint degree programs and joint faculties, introduction of new education directions and specialties, reintroduction of evening departments, introduction of university autonomy on student quotas and education programs according to labor market estimates, and recognition of diplomas obtained abroad, among others.

Until recently, Uzbekistan had the lowest proportion of school-leavers entering higher education, at just 9%.[106] There are several reasons for the low participation rate. First, the government limited enrollment by applying strict quotas until 2017. Second, almost half of Uzbekistan's 85 higher education institutions were in the capital city, which made it difficult for rural students to access higher education. To resolve the situation, the total number of higher education institutions was increased from 77 in 2016 to 95 in 2018; 16 joint programs were introduced in cooperation with overseas universities. Students quotas for overall admission to higher education have been doubled.[107]

Since the reforms, almost all higher education institutions have been reorganized to offer 4-year bachelor degrees, 2-year master degrees, and doctoral programs. The current intake is about 63,000 students and about 25% graduate each year from university; more than 90% graduate with bachelor degrees. Affordability of tertiary education is a challenge. More than 50% of students in higher education come from households in the top consumption quintile, which suggests barriers to financial accessibility of higher education. Almost 70% of undergraduates and 75% of graduate students pay their fees through individual contracts. Since school year 2017–2018, universities have been allowed to admit additional students at a higher contract rate called the "super contract." Additional admission is executed in accordance with the order of applicants who do not have the required number of points to be admitted on a regular contract basis, and their willingness to pay the higher contract rates. The introduction of the "super contract" will increase the gap in affordability and access to higher education for students from households in the lower consumption quintiles.

Although there is no legal obligation to find employment for all graduates, the higher education system helps as many graduates as possible find jobs. An institution organizes regular meetings and activities with the participation of potential employers, ensures participation of employers during the final examination, and organizes job fairs with local authorities. Higher education institutions collect data on the employment of graduates and annually report the data to the ministry.

According to UNESCO, "continued vocational education and training (CVET) opportunities are limited in Uzbekistan. Provision of CVET decreased significantly after the dissolution of the Soviet Union when many training centers serving SOEs closed. With higher demand for skilled workers from the private sector, CVET provision is

---

[106] Higher education refers to post-upper secondary level (beyond grade 11), including vocational training colleges and bachelor programs.
[107] This and the following sections are based on European Commission. 2017. *Overview of the Higher Education System—Uzbekistan*. Brussels. and footnote 95.

now predominantly company-based. The public education and training system does not recognize the training delivered by enterprises as it cannot assess the quality of training that does not comply with formal curricula. The notion of continuing education is largely applied as formal education, mainly for people to upgrade their qualifications or to requalify" (footnote 95).

In 2017, however, the Cabinet adopted a resolution, On Measures to Establish Vocational Training Centers for Unemployed Citizens in the Territory of Uzbekistan. As a result, 11 vocational training centers are being planned for the unemployed in all regions of the country.

IV. ADB in Central Asia

ADB has broad portfolio of engagements in Central Asia. In education and TVET, Tajikistan and the Kyrgyz Republic are the principal partners of ADB.

A. Tajikistan

Grant 0452/Grant 0453 /Loan 3309-TAJ: Strengthening Technical and Vocational Education and Training

The expected impact of the project is a national workforce with an increased proportion of skilled workers employed in Tajikistan. The outcome will be a demand-driven, quality-assured, and flexible technical and vocational education and training (TVET) system responsive to labor market needs.

The project has four outputs: (i) TVET system methodology modernized, (ii) physical learning facilities in selected TVET institutions upgraded, (iii) access to quality TVET programs improved, and (iv) governance and management of TVET system strengthened.

Output 1. TVET system methodology modernized. The project has developed competency standards and assessment tools aligned to an adapted European Qualification Framework. Competency-based training (CBT) curriculum and gender-sensitive learning materials will be developed and competency assessors for 17 occupations trained. The occupations were selected based on the government's development priorities, a labor market survey conducted during project preparation, and inputs from key stakeholders. An implementation plan for the development of the CBT components was developed involving industry sector working groups, training providers, and development partners. Guidelines and manuals were prepared to promote future sustainability and institutionalize tasks related to development of competency standards, qualifications, and curriculum. The Center for Training Methodology and Monitoring of Education Quality under the Ministry of Labor, Migration and Employment (Ministry of Labor, Migration and Employment) has the lead in implementing output 1. The CBT curriculum and learning materials are being piloted in 29 TVET institutions.

Output 2. Physical learning facilities in selected TVET institutions upgraded. The project is upgrading the physical learning and teaching facilities of selected TVET institutions. The design of rehabilitation works considers teaching requirements, student needs, and environmental and social safeguards. In three project sites, green reconstruction and power approaches will demonstrate options for general building rehabilitation and help train teachers and students in green reconstruction. The project supports gender-appropriate dormitory upgrades, which will help increase female access to formal TVET.

Output 3. Access to quality TVET programs improved. The project is developing an in-service TVET teacher training plan to provide teachers and master trainers with a clear understanding of the CBT methodology, competencies in student-centered training delivery, and practical knowledge and skills in technology areas through industry internships.

Output 4. Governance and management strengthened. The project is supporting the establishment and operation of industry advisory committees and working groups in the five priority sectors; training in modern TVET management; strengthening of the secretariat of the National Coordination Council for Vocational Education and Training; provision of equipment for the Scientific Research Institute on Labor, Migration and Employment under Ministry of Labor, Migration and Employment to support annual labor market assessments; and implementation of the project monitoring and evaluation system.

Dates:	April 2016–September 2021 (extended to March 2022)
Budget:	ADB: $30 million
	Clean Energy Fund under the Clean Energy Financing Partnership Facility: $2 million

Grant 0714-TAJ and Grant 9207-TAJ: Skills and Employability Enhancement Project

The project will have the following outcome: skills and employability of youth, women, and labor migrants for domestic and overseas labor market improved.

The project has three outputs:

Output 1. More inclusive and targeted migration support provided. To reduce the risks of migration for youth and help them find better jobs, the project will establish and equip three migration service centers that will provide (i) a predeparture orientation program, (ii) a preemployment program, (iii) a new information and communication technology (ICT) literacy program, (iv) a pilot for behavioral change initiatives for migrants and migrant families, and (v) job counselling services for returning migrant workers. The centers will offer one-stop service centers to departing and returning migrants.

Output 2. Access to and relevance of public employment services enhanced. To provide better service to youth and female jobs seekers, the project will establish and equip three model job centers that will provide (i) enhanced comprehensive employment services, including skills training; (ii) childcare centers and a pilot stipend program for female job seekers; (iii) a pilot program of new and more focused soft skills training; (iv) job counselling services to match interests and skills to potential jobs; and (v) ICT skills training programs for selected sectors. Job centers with dormitories will be built and equipped in Dushanbe for tourism, in Rogun for energy, and in Dangara for agriculture. Job centers will provide skills training for selected occupations in the three targeted sectors. Training programs will be developed based on the competency-based training approach. Job counselling will be provided using updated ICT equipment and new aptitude testing software.

Output 3. Planning and management of migration and employment services strengthened. To provide better service to youth and female job seekers and migrant youth workers, the project will (i) develop a new national classification of occupations (NCO) based on ISCO-08 and help apply the NCO to training certifications and labor market surveys, (ii) pilot a skills and employment survey for tourism, (iii) expand the labor market portal under the Ministry of Labor, Migration and Employment and undertake client job center tracking surveys, (iv) provide training for Ministry of Labor, Migration and Employment and the migration and employment agency, (v) promote awareness of migration and employment services, and (vi) strengthen the adult learning centers' capacity to certify training programs. A large-scale tracer study of the beneficiaries of job centers will assess the project impact.

Dates:	June 2020–March 2027
Budget:	ADB: $30 million
	Japan Fund for Information and Communication Technology: $1.5 million

B. Kyrgyz Republic

TA 4672-KGZ: Vocational Education and Skills Training Project

The technical assistance (TA) helped prepare a project that will improve access to and quality and relevance of demand-driven vocational education and skills training (VEST) for youth and adults. The TA addressed the issues mentioned and prepared a project that will (i) rationalize the current VEST system and build the capacity required to stimulate relevance, equity, flexibility, and efficiency of primary vocational education, including upgrading and rehabilitating selected training facilities; (ii) increase skills training and retraining opportunities for adults; and (iii) strengthen public–private partnerships by expanding linkages between the supply of VEST and labor market needs.

Dates:	November 2005–January 2007
Budget:	$300,000

Grant 0074-KGZ: Vocational Education and Skills Development

The project helped the government reform primary vocational education (PVE) and increase skills training opportunities for adults and out-of-school youth. The project had four components: (i) consolidating the PVE system, (ii) improving the teaching and learning environment, (iii) modernizing curricula and assessment and developing learning materials, and (iv) developing human resources.

Dates:	February 2008–April 2013
Budget:	$10 million

TA 9212-KGZ: Skilling and Entrepreneurship for Inclusive Growth Sector Development Program

The technical assistance was intended to design a project that produced technical and vocational education and training graduates with skills that increasingly matched the current and future job market's need for highly skilled workers, thus reducing unemployment among skilled youth and transforming them into the working nonpoor.

Dates:	November 2016–December 2018
Budget:	$750,000

Grant 0552-KGZ and Grant 0553-KGZ: Skills for Inclusive Growth Sector Development Program

The program is aligned with government strategies to achieve inclusive growth through improved workforce skills and productivity in key economic sectors, specifically the National Sustainable Development Strategy, 2013–2017; the Education Development Strategy, 2012–2020; and the Regional Policy of the Kyrgyz Republic, 2018–2022. The program will have the following outcome: an established market-responsive, entrepreneurial, and inclusive technical and vocational education and training (TVET) system. The program includes three outputs: (i) TVET governance and finance strengthened, (ii) teaching quality and learning environments improved, and (iii) cooperation with industry increased and entrepreneurship skills developed.

Dates:	December 2017–December 2021
Budget:	$30 million

C. Uzbekistan

TA 9256-UZB: Skills Strategies for Industrial Modernization and Inclusive Growth

The government requested support from the Asian Development Bank (ADB) to support the country's transformation into a modern industrial and service economy through sustained and inclusive growth, reduced poverty, and expanded regional cooperation.

The government is pursuing an ambitious development agenda to modernize the economy and to achieve rapid and broad-based economic growth through economic diversification, industrial modernization, and infrastructure development. The skills development system faces several challenges and is not well placed to support the government's economic modernization agenda. Employers report that inadequate workforce skills pose a significant obstacle to firms' growth.

Dates:	January 2017–November 2020
Budget:	$900,000

TA 9727-UZB: Preparing the Skills Development for a Modern Economy Project

The project aimed to increase jobs, particularly for youth. It provided investment finance to help students and job seekers learn market-driven skills by (i) improving employment and workforce development services, (ii) enhancing quality and relevance of skills development, and (iii) strengthening sector governance and management.

Dates:	May 2019–April 2021
Budget:	$720,000

V. Many Challenges Remain

To varying degrees, the five countries have launched important education reforms, including in TVET, to overcome weaknesses inherited from the Soviet era. The reforms' common feature is a desire to bring education more in line with economic needs and opportunities and to optimize the use of available resources. However, important challenges remain. This chapter summarizes some of them, especially in TVET.

A. Technical and Vocational Education and Training Governance and Management

All the countries are transitioning from centralized to decentralized governance and management of TVET and higher education. In all the countries, several ministries are responsible for school education, TVET, higher education, adult education, and human resource development.

In Tajikistan, TVET remains disjointed and uncoordinated. The competition between Ministry of Labor, Migration and Employment and Ministry of Education and Science is holding back all harmonization initiatives. The division of responsibility between Ministry of Labor, Migration and Employment and Ministry of Education and Science has been a cause of debate and conflict ever since IVET was separated from technical secondary education and transferred to Ministry of Labor, Migration and Employment. Ministry of Education and Science is mandated to secure the quality of TVET and higher education and to ensure that assessment, certification, and accreditation take place in a fair and transparent manner. It is Ministry of Education and Science' responsibility to assure the quality of all TVET institutions. Resource limitations mean that this only partially takes place. The absence of commonly accepted occupational standards for TVET and higher education further complicates the quality assurance process. The fact that TVET regulatory functions and responsibility for TVET provision are embedded in the same organizational structures contribute to the lack of transparency and accountability. In an increasing number of countries, these functions are separated.

In Turkmenistan, because of the fragmentation of VET across different sectoral ministries and the Ministry of Education, the progression routes of qualifications are not well defined. There is no coordination among the different TVET subsystems.

The governance and management of TVET can be improved in several ways: (i) establish management boards or advisory committees with external participation at each TVET institution; (ii) delegate more responsibility to the management of TVET institutions, i.e., control over the budget and the right to hire and fire staff; and (iii) introduce an electronic management information system for TVET to store relevant data concerning students and their performance, teaching staff, and TVET institutions' facilities. A TVET management information system will create a basis for improved assessment of learning outcomes.

B. Responsiveness of Technical and Vocational Education and Training System

The steady and often rapid changes to national economies caused by external factors, such as the global crisis and the impact of climate change, require that countries be able to respond rapidly to the emerging situation, including to adjust the balance between the supply of and demand for skilled labor.

LMIS is a useful tool for matching the supply and demand for skills. None of the five countries have fully developed LMISs, but Uzbekistan and the Kyrgyz Republic have adopted frequent tracer studies to measure the relevance of TVET and higher education. In Tajikistan, the labor market and the absorption of graduates is not systematically monitored. Skills audits and tracer studies are well-known instruments for this purpose.

Labor market responsiveness, however, goes beyond labor market monitoring. Efficient TVET requires that the different levels of the system be capable of responding to the information available, i.e., to phase out programs with little demand and introduce new ones asked for. This is possible only if TVET and higher education have a high level of flexibility.

In Tajikistan, links to the private sector are extremely weak, except for a few vocational lyceums and TVET colleges. IVET lyceums, especially, have limited readiness to strengthen interaction with prospective employers; Ministry of Labor, Migration and Employment has pointed this out as a weakness of IVET. The management of secondary TVET colleges appears to have a better understanding of the importance of intensifying links to private companies. The fact that the private sector is poorly organized and essentially unable to articulate its skills needs complicates the situation. A result of the limited contact is lack of alignment of existing TVET content to the needs and opportunities of the labor market. Efforts have been made to establish councils at the vocational lyceums with external participation. So far, however, the response has been limited.

Partnership with employers in the productive sectors, whether private or public, is essential for a well-functioning TVET and higher education system. There are several potential avenues for partnerships: (i) cofinancing of selected TVET and higher education programs, (ii) employers' participation in curriculum development and assessment of graduates, (iii) joint research and development activities, (iv) internships and apprenticeship arrangements, (v) establishment of sector skills councils, and (vi) employment participation in the governance of TVET and higher education institutions. All these avenues are at an early stage of development in the countries.

C. Quality and Relevance of Technical and Vocational Education and Training

Most reform initiatives in Central Asia have focused more on access and inclusiveness than quality of education. The situation has contributed to the shortage of qualified workers who, in addition to technical skills, do not have foreign language skills, management skills, and transversal competencies. Continuous training for adults is restricted to professional development. There is no funding for nonformal adult education, except for training opportunities for the unemployed and professional development for teachers and civil servants, which are paid for by employers, government, and nongovernment organizations.

As a result of resource constraints, most TVET institutions in Central Asia, except Kazakhstan, are in serious need of improvement. The Tajik National Strategy for Education Development articulates the serious situation of many TVET institutions: (i) acute shortage of industry training specialists, (ii) low qualification level of teachers, (iii) nonconformity of TVET graduates with labor market requirements, (iv) lack of up-to-date education and methodical training materials and equipment, (v) employers and other social partners insufficiently involved in the training system, (vi) no mechanism to attract private sector financial resources for vocational education and staff development, and (vii) lack of training in business and job search skills to help graduates ensure they are employed or start their own business. In Tajikistan, the situation is more critical for IVET centers and ALCs than for technical colleges. As a result of the closure of most SOEs, students have lost the opportunity to acquire practical skills associated with their trade, a challenge still calling for a solution. Donor support to the sector has eased these deficiencies only to a limited extent.

In the Kyrgyz Republic, only a fraction of the many vocational occupations and specializations are taught because of the shortage of qualified teaching staff, scarcity of equipment, and outdated curricula.

Low quality and labor market relevance of VET have several implications. First, public and private employers have difficulty recruiting qualified people. Second, TVET is less attractive to the young, who opt for the academic stream of upper secondary education and higher education instead of IVET and secondary TVET.

D. Shortage of Jobs

Except in Kazakhstan, unemployment and underemployment are serious concerns. The Uzbekistan economy creates about 280,000 new jobs per year on average (on a net basis) compared with the 600,000 annual entrants to the labor market. The economy needs to double the number of jobs created each year just to absorb new entrants. Most jobs will have to be created by establishing new firms and some by expanding existing firms. Other structural challenges are skills gaps and a limited supply of training in technical skills, high youth unemployment, high economic inactivity and long-term unemployment, and limited labor mobility.

Tajikistan's working-age population (15–75 years old) is about 5.3 million, of whom 2.4 million are economically active. Years of strong economic growth in the last decade have not translated into sufficient job creation. In 2003–2013, the economy added fewer than 500,000 jobs. Real GDP grew by an average of 7.2% per year, as employment expanded by about 2.1% per year, implying average employment-to-growth elasticity of about 0.3, equal to the averages of Central Asia and lower-middle-income countries. The jobs that were created domestically were mainly in agriculture (62%) and services (20%), sectors with low productivity, while industry shed as many jobs as construction created. The number of public sector jobs has fallen since the 1990s because of privatization efforts, but the share of total employment in government institutions and SOEs is still about 25%. As a result, while an average of 160,000[108] young people enter the labor force each year, not more than an estimated 50,000–60,000 formal sector job openings are available every year. Instead, many entrants to the labor market join the informal economy, which is highly insecure because of the lack of regulation and enforcement of legislation.

The situation calls for (i) efforts to further diversify the economy, which would make countries less dependent on labor migration; and (ii) intensified use of so-called active labor market programs (ALMPs) such as job placement assistance to school-leavers, wage subsidies, and start-up support to talented youth.

---

[108] Different sources have different estimates of the number of young people entering the labor market.

E. School-to-Work Transition

Tajikistan. The education system produces a high number of secondary school graduates, who have serious problems finding a stable job, as indicated by the high share of secondary school graduates in the informal sector and among migrant workers. No reliable data on the labor market absorption of secondary TVET and higher education graduates exist, but available sources suggest that they have less difficulty finding a formal sector job than secondary graduates. A surprisingly high number of higher education graduates, however, are engaged in the informal sector, for instance, as taxi drivers. Most have a degree in a "soft" area. With regard to IVET, the picture is more complex. Clearly, vocational lyceums are far from fulfilling their role as the main source of skilled professionals for the productive sectors. The sketchy evidence available suggests that most graduates pursue further education, while those entering the labor market mostly end up in the informal sector or go abroad. Interviews with employers indicate that they find that IVET graduates lack practical and cognitive competencies. Although the salary expectations of secondary TVET and higher education graduates are higher, employers prefer them, provided they have the right specialization. However, ongoing investments in IVET by ADB and the EU may change this situation.

Turkmenistan. The narrowness of the education pyramid means that only 7% of secondary education graduates make it to higher education, while about 15% continue their education at a secondary VET school. As a result, more than 75% of secondary education or IVET graduates enter the labor market.

Kyrgyz Republic. Changes in the country's economic structure and lack of skilled labor, combined with the predominance of children and young people (33% of the population), call for reforms in education so that it can equip learners with cognitive skills and transversal competencies.

Career counselling and guidance can ease the school-to-work transition. Experience suggests that they are particularly important for TVET and higher education programs as informed students are more responsive to labor market opportunities. All the countries lack proper career guidance or orientation systems. Lack of experienced career counsellors and computer-based information programs represents a major bottleneck that prevents effective career choice by young people and adults, as well as a smooth transition from training to the labor market (footnote 95).

F. Distance Education and E-learning

Distance education supported by ICT recently started in Central Asia and shows great potential in building lifelong systems. E-learning could expand access to quality learning at all levels of education, especially in the large number of small schools (ungraded classrooms) in several countries. E-learning systems have a positive impact on the learning process and on the quality of teaching, paving the way for lifelong learning through their usability (footnote 95). The COVID-19 outbreak has accentuated the importance of developing e-learning as a supplement to conventional classroom-based learning.

In Tajikistan, ICT-supported distance learning is still underdeveloped and needs to be introduced in higher and secondary vocational education.

G. Regional Coordination and Collaboration

Despite CAREC's plan to create a cluster on human development, there are no formal regional structures for coordination among authorities dealing with TVET. Limited bilateral collaboration between countries is taking place. As regards labor migration, Kazakhstan and the Kyrgyz Republic collaborate through the Eurasian Economic Union.

VI. Recommendations for Future Technical and Vocational Education and Training Engagements

This chapter presents examples of international good practices in selected areas.

A. Increasing the Technical and Vocational Education and Training System's Responsiveness

The most serious challenge faced by education systems is the mismatch between the needs and opportunities of the labor market and the qualifications of graduates, whether of TVET or higher education.

TVET and higher education must be able to respond to changing demand for different types of skills (e.g., by introducing new courses in new areas of demand and phasing out courses in occupational areas where employment prospects are poor). Becoming responsive requires systemic flexibility to smoothly adjust to such changes and a degree of autonomy for TVET institutions. However, the basis for this is the ability to identify demand for different categories of skills and competencies.

Identification of Labor Market Trends

There are three basic mechanisms for identifying skills needs and jobs: (i) fora for dialogue between TVET and higher education institutions and employers, e.g., skills councils or advisory boards at the level of the individual institution; (ii) skills audits, which are enterprise-based surveys that collect information about job vacancies, skills shortages, and forecasts about demand for labor; and (iii) tracer studies of graduates.

However, the ultimate success criterion is that TVET and higher education can translate this information into more labor market–relevant course offerings.

Tracer studies. Tracer studies can give especially important information about skills matching by combining objective and subjective data from graduates (Box 2). Apart from being able to measure the employability of graduates and obtain feedback to improve study programs, tracer studies allow aspects of horizontal matching (relevance of the field of study for tasks done in the job) and vertical matching (appropriate position regarding the level of formal qualification) to be measured.

Improvement of collection of labor market information. LMISs are useful for matching the supply of skills with employer demand and opportunities for self-employment, and for guiding students and job seekers. Information about major industries, recent growth areas, occupations experiencing shortages, qualifications needed for jobs, and so on, can help people make better-informed choices about their education and careers.

Box 2: Tracer Studies

Tracer studies can help answer questions such as the following:
(i) What happens to graduates after leaving the education institution?
(ii) Were they able to get paid employment in an acceptable time?
(iii) Do they use the skills and competencies they have acquired in their education or training? If not, why?
(iv) What are the skills and competencies required by the labor market?

Tracer studies are flexible tools that allow combining a core questionnaire, where key elements are systematically asked, with ad hoc modules that allow information on aspects that are important at one point in time, or that are important for concrete institutions (or fields of study).

Tracer studies may be conducted either as a centralized exercise with a national or regional scope or as a decentralized exercise with focus on a specific TVET or higher education institution. For centralized tracer studies, the main objective is to inform ministries and other central bodies about the graduates' labor market success. The studies normally use the same questionnaire for all institutions. Decentralized tracer studies primarily serve as a management tool, allowing management to get a better sense of the quality and relevance of the programs offered.

Tracer studies are usually conducted 6 or 12 months after graduation, depending on the nature of the education and training program to be evaluated.

Source: European Training Foundation. 2017. *Tracer Studies. Evaluating the Impact of Training Programs.* Torino.

Many countries have established LMISs to systematize the collection and sharing of labor market data. An LMIS is a system to store, disseminate, and use labor market-related information and results. The functions of an LMIS include (i) information sharing among labor market actors and institutions, (ii) monitoring of labor market trends, and (iii) guidance of students and their parents.

A national system for classification of occupations based on international standards, e.g., ISCO-08, would ease the analysis of labor market information.

Box 3: Labor Market Information

Most labor market information systems (LMISs) build on three types of intelligence: (i) administrative data such as enrollment in and graduation from different types of education and training programs, and number of registered job seekers and advertised employment opportunities; (ii) statistics, surveys, and studies, including labor force surveys, tracer studies, migration data, sector skills audits; and (iii) observations and advice by different stakeholders such as business associations.

In some countries, the LMIS is used as a portal where youth can seek information on education and career opportunities (Jamaica) and job openings (Singapore) and as an online application for registration of employers (Uttar Pradesh, India).

It is essential that responsibility for management of the LMIS be well defined and the quality of the collected data critically assessed.

Source: International Labour Organization. (www.Labour market information systems (LMIS) - ILOSTAT).

Implementation of these measures requires building capacity in data collection, data analysis, and utilization and interpretation of results to improve policy, TVET institutes, and financing. An LMIS needs to be complemented by coordination among key TVET stakeholders, including industry, to ensure timely reaction to changing local skills requirements.

B. Quality and Efficiency of Technical and Vocational Education and Training

Quality Management

After a decade of focusing on expanding the capacity of the education system, the countries are increasingly paying attention to the quality of TVET and higher education. However, raising education quality requires well-functioning procedures for quality management, including assessment, certification, and accreditation.

In all the countries, responsibility for the TVET streams is divided between ministries and authorities. The division hampers coordination and creates unclear lines of progression within the education system, which, in turn, lead to suboptimal utilization of existing resources. Creation of a national authority responsible for all TVET streams has proved effective in securing a more homogenous system and enabling more even allocation of resources among institutions. Such authorities have been established in several countries, including Australia, Maldives, and Singapore. Typically, the authority deals with development of curricula and assessment criteria, certification of TVET institutions, labor market monitoring, and policy development related to TVET (Box 4). The advantage of this model is that it separates regulation and quality control from the delivery of TVET programs.

Education Management

An education management information system (EMIS) collects, integrates, processes, maintains, and disseminates data and information to support decision-making, policy analysis and formulation, planning, monitoring, and management at all levels of an education system (Box 5). An EMIS can be used by schools, TVET institutions, and universities. An EMIS can be implemented at a group level, comprising multiple institutions operating under the same structure, or even at a government level for hundreds of schools and TVET institutions under a regional administration or ministry. Although an EMIS is an important management tool, its use is limited in Central Asia.

Management Capacity of Technical and Vocational Education and Training Institutions

A well-functioning, demand-responsive TVET system requires institutions that are managed by competent people capable of responding flexibly to labor market changes and maintaining constructive dialogue with local partners. Few managers and administrators have such qualifications. Capacity-building initiatives providing such expertise are essential to strengthen the effectiveness and efficiency of TVET.

Technical and Vocational Education and Teacher Training

In Central Asia and many other countries, TVET teachers and instructors do not commonly possess a strong background in working in industry and lack familiarity with new technologies. Many lack enthusiasm to collaborate with industry. Many TVET teachers have limited knowledge about modern teaching methodologies such as the use of technology-powered learning devices.

Box 4: Australia Skills Quality Authority

The Australia Skills Quality Authority (ASQA) is the national regulator for vocational education and training. Under the National Vocational Education and Training Regulator Act 2011, ASQA has the following functions:

(i) Register an organization as a training organization.
(ii) Accredit courses that may be offered and/or provided by registered training organizations (RTOs).
(iii) Carry out compliance audit activities of RTOs.
(iv) Promote and encourage the continuous improvement of an RTO's capacity to provide VET courses or part of VET courses.
(v) Advise and make recommendations to the minister on matters relating to VET.
(vi) Advise and make recommendations to the minister responsible for training in a state or territory on specific matters relating to VET in the state or territory.
(vii) Advise and make recommendations to the Ministerial Council on general matters relating to VET in all jurisdictions.
(viii) Collect, analyze, interpret, and disseminate information about VET.
(ix) Publish performance information, of a kind prescribed by the National Vocational Education and Training Regulations 2011, relating to RTOs.
(x) Conduct training programs relating to the regulation of RTOs and/or the accreditation of courses.
(xi) Enter arrangements with occupational licensing bodies, other industry bodies, or both, to ensure compliance by RTOs with the National Vocational Education and Training Regulator Act.
(xii) Cooperate with a regulatory authority of another country that has responsibility for the quality or regulation of VET for all or part of the country.
(xiii) Develop relationships with counterparts in other countries.

ASQA has established a stakeholder liaison group to engage and consult with providers and other key stakeholders on ASQA's approach to engagement and education and to identify and respond to key issues facing providers. Industry stakeholders that ASQA engages with include skills service organizations, industry regulators and licensing bodies, peak industry and employer groups, and other government agencies.

ASQA is an independent statutory authority, accountable to Parliament, and is headed by a governor-general.

Source: Australian Skills Quality Authority. www.asqu.gov.au.

Box 5: Technical and Vocational Education and Training Management Information System, South Africa

The Technical and Vocational Education and Training Management Information System (TVETMIS) is a unit record-based information system that stores and maintains unit records of technical and vocational education and training college data related to colleges and their campuses, programs, subjects, staff, and students. The data content of TVETMIS is primarily maintained and supplied by TVET colleges by means of electronic data submission files that are extracted in standard formats and transmitted to the Department of Higher Education and Training to be loaded into TVETMIS.

Source: Department of Higher Education. webapps.dhet.gov.za/TECHNICA.

> **Box 6: Turkey—Continuing Professional Development for Technical and Vocational Education and Training Teachers**
>
> There is diverse public and private sector provision of various kinds of continuing professional development (CPD) for vocational education and training (VET) teachers, and capacity has expanded in response to policy and to funding. CPD opportunities for TVET teachers provided by the main national and international stakeholders range from pedagogical to human resource management to strictly technical and vocational subjects. Public and private training institutes; major industrial companies such as Ford, Oyak-Renault, TOFAŞ-Fiat, Mercedes-Benz, Hyundai, Toyota, and Vestel; universities; nongovernment organizations; and other third-sector organizations make short-cycle and long-cycle formal and nonformal training courses available. Online resources, such as EdX, Coursera, the Khan Academy, and Turkcell Akademi are available.
>
> Universities provide CPD for VET teachers through continuing education centers in areas requiring specific academic and high technical skills. Opportunities for practical training in industry, which usually exist where school–industry linkages are strong, are especially welcomed by the teachers and trainers.
>
> The Ministry of National Education is the key player in CPD for VET teachers and instructors. In addition to its main role in initial teacher training, the Council of Higher Education through universities is also a leading provider of CPD for VET teachers and trainers. The ministry strongly encourages and regulates additional provision of CPD for teachers through other means, for example, protocols with training organizations, companies, and donors.
>
> Source: European Training Foundation. 2016. *Continuing Professional Development for Vocational Teachers and Trainers in Turkey*. Torino.

All the countries have procedures and institutions dealing with preservice training of technical teachers. However, because of unattractive employment conditions, including low salaries, most of the countries struggle with the challenge of underqualified and unmotivated staff. Often, wages in industry are significantly higher than those offered by the public TVET system. Upskilling of teachers and instructors already employed is an area calling for attention.

Collaboration with industry allowing teachers and instructors to update their practical skills at a workplace has proved to be a fruitful solution to this situation (Box 6). Another possibility is to invite technical staff members from industry to teach at the TVET institution. For higher education institutions, strategic partnerships with enterprises have shown promising results, at times linked to joint research activities. Some countries have good experiences allowing teaching staff to engage in supplementary activities to compensate for low salaries.

C. Public–Private Partnerships and Industry Partnerships

PPPs in TVET can be of two types: (i) collaboration between public training institutions and private enterprises, or (ii) twinning arrangements between public and private training institutions. The term can also refer to the involvement of private sector representatives in the development of TVET programs and in governance and management of TVET.

PPPs in TVET are a common feature in most industrialized and middle-income countries, although the operational details vary across industries and countries. The advantages of PPPs are obvious. They reduce the financial burden on the government and narrow the gap between the skills taught and the skills asked for by private companies. When TVET is provided by a company with production facilities, the trainee's employment prospects increase. However, PPPs require that government authorities be capable of fulfilling their regulatory and supervisory responsibilities.

Industry engagement options include identification of skills gaps, development of competency standards, delivery of training at the workplace, examination, certification, joint research, provision of equipment and facilities, management of TVET institutions, and governance.

Lessons learned from existing PPPs suggest that, to avoid potential conflicts of interest, adequate legislation must be in place and relationships must be regulated by clearly defined responsibilities and rights between the two sides. On the government side, the necessary legal expertise must be available and the legal system ready to enforce the legislation as intended.

Box 7: Siemens Technical Academy, Mumbai, India

The Siemens Technical Academy (STA) was started in 2015 to provide work-integrated training to underprivileged students. They need to score at least 60% in their 10th standard to qualify for the courses. STA offers courses for fitters and electricians. It has a tie-up with Tata STRIVE to implement the dual vocational education and training (VET) methodology, which mandates 80% practical exposure with industry engagement. The students are engaged as apprentices and receive a stipend for their daily expenses. At the end of the 2-year course, the students get a National Council for Vocational Training certification at National Skills Qualification Framework level 5.

Students get a chance to apply their learning through innovative projects in 3D printing, SMART lighting, and robotics. At the end of the course, students are placed in Siemens or its partners or they choose to apply elsewhere.

Besides post-training placements, students are exposed to various aspects of a rigorous earn-while-you-learn apprentice scheme.

Features of the STA include the following:
(i) Curriculum and methodology are globally proven and integrated with technology of the future by following pedagogic principles of project-based immersive learning.
(ii) The modularity of the curriculum ensures seamless integration of theory and practice with 80% focus on hands-on learning.
(iii) Emphasis on problem solving and interpersonal skills initiates the students into lifelong learning.
(iv) Since the youth are from diverse economic backgrounds, the training approach is sensitive to sociocultural elements.
(v) The commitment of firms is assured since they are keen to invest in a future-ready workforce and restore the dignity of skills.
(vi) Digitally aided classrooms and instructors and mentors who are highly skilled and motivated guide and supervise the students.
(vii) Workshop equipment exposes the students to real work scenarios and prepares them for the world of work with zero tolerance for defects, cost-efficiency, and resource management.
(viii) Dual VET certification is of high repute and attracts higher remuneration, besides being recognized by industries.
(ix) Students have options to build a long-term career through many paths that can lead to employment or entrepreneurship.

Source: Team NSN. 2018. Siemens Technical Academy (STA), Mumbai—German Dual VET Transforms the Lives of Youth in India. National Skills Network. 8 October.

Box 8: Vocational and Metallurgical College under the Tajik Aluminum Company

The Tajik Aluminum Company (TALCO) fully operates and maintains the specialized metallurgical college to train technician professionals and hire them. TALCO actively participates in the development of the content of education programs, training curricula, and assessment of students' competencies. TALCO provides a job to each graduate. Students undergo practical training and workshops at the facilities of the enterprise for at least 70% of the total number of training hours. The salary of the instructors is equal to that of professionals and staff of the company. TALCO uses former and current employees as mentors and instructors.

Source: Information provided by Ministry of Labor, Migration and Employment. 2020.

D. Easing School-to-Work Transition

Although official youth unemployment is relatively low in most Central Asian countries, school-to-work transition remains a challenge. Many young people enter the labor market with completed secondary education as their only qualification, and for those with a TVET or higher education qualification, many work outside their area of expertise. The considerable number of people engaged in informal sector activities in most of the countries indicates that underemployment is prevalent. More attention should be paid to the school-to-work transition.

Career Guidance and Counselling

Career guidance is defined as the services that help people of any age manage their careers and make the right education, training, and occupational choices. Career guidance involves a range of connected activities, including provision of career information, personalized guidance and counselling, skills assessment, engagement with the world of work, and teaching of decision-making and career management skills. Career guidance is delivered face to face, by telephone, and online. Ideally, career guidance is continuous and lifelong. It is critical to the smooth transition of young people as they make choices about education and training and to the mobility and (re)engagement of adults in the labor market. Guidance is provided to people in a wide range of settings: schools and training centers; tertiary and higher education institutions; employment services and career guidance centers; workplaces, trade unions, and professional bodies; and local community settings.[109]

Specific measures might include the establishment of career guidance centers at TVET and higher education institutions, training of career advisors, and creation of a website (portal) where students and their parents can seek information concerning education and jobs.

Entrepreneurship Development

Few young people consider entrepreneurship as an option; they find self-employment less attractive than being a wage earner.[110] Those who start their own business mostly operate informally on a small scale and lack ambition (and ability) to expand the business.

---

[109] European Centre for the Development of Vocational Training. https://www.cedefop.europa.eu/en.
[110] Entrepreneurs refer to business owners who are motivated to develop their own business, thereby creating jobs for others.

A considerable amount of untapped entrepreneurship potential is believed to exist in all the countries. Stimulating entrepreneurship among young people is relevant mainly for IVET and higher education graduates. Measures available to them include establishing business advisory centers and incubator facilities at selected training centers and colleges, coaching start-ups, following up on ad hoc training, and linking potential entrepreneurs to microcredit institutions. Experience suggests that basic business management training has limited effect if not combined with other support services.

Box 9: Singapore—Education and Career Guidance

Education and Career Guidance (ECG) is a holistic and experiential effort by SkillsFuture to equip students and adults with the knowledge, skills, and values to make informed education and career decisions.

ECG users are encouraged to learn more about their own interests, abilities, and passions. By exploring the learning or education pathways and career opportunities available across different industries, users can take positive steps toward realizing their aspirations and embrace lifelong learning.

ECG supports individuals at different life stages—from the early schooling years and throughout their working life.

Primary, secondary, junior college, and centralized institute students go through an ECG curriculum that meets their developmental needs at different stages. On top of education planning and career exploration programs and activities, the interactive MySkillsFuture website (for primary 5–6 students, secondary students, and pre-university students) helps students discover their strengths and interests and provides information on industries, occupations, courses, and education institutions in Singapore. Teachers, who are the first touch points with students, have been equipped with basic ECG knowledge to support students.

For students requiring more dedicated support, ECG counsellors in public schools provide individual counselling or group guidance in education and career choices. Aside from supporting and collaborating with personnel to drive and facilitate the provision of quality ECG experiences for students, counsellors communicate and engage with parents and industry partners where required.

Institute of Technical Education and polytechnic students. A minimum of 40–60 hours over 2 years for Institute of Technical Education (ITE) students and 3 years for polytechnic students have been set aside for ECG, and ITE and all polytechnics have been resourced with ECG counsellors. As in schools, lecturers are the first touch points with students at ITE and the polytechnics and are equipped with basic ECG knowledge. As part of an immersive ECG experience, students engage in ECG-related activities and lessons in the classroom and participate in out-of-classroom activities such as industry immersion programs, learning journeys, and career talks. These activities help them continue developing skills to make informed career decisions and prepare them for a smooth transition into the workplace. Students can meet with ECG counsellors in small groups or through individual appointments.

Students from the publicly funded universities can access career counselling services and preparation programs that will help them identify and prepare for careers related to their strengths, interests, and fields of study. The services and programs are provided by dedicated career service offices or centers on campus.

Adults may access career advisory services through Workforce Singapore's Careers Connect. New workforce entrants, mid-career switchers, or those in career transition can benefit from the suite of career matching services, which are tailored to job seekers' needs. Services include career advice, job search workshops, and interactive career resources. Those who require more in-depth help may receive one-to-one career coaching from professionally certified career coaches.

Source: SkillsFuture.

Active Labor Market Programs

Active Labor Market Programs (ALMPs) mainly aim to increase jobs and improve matching between jobs (vacancies) and workers (i.e., the unemployed).[111] ALMP instruments range from vocational training to indirect employment incentives (e.g., job retention, job sharing, recruitment subsidies) to setting up sheltered and supported employment or directly creating jobs (i.e., public work schemes) and providing start-up incentives. When planned and implemented well, ALMPs are useful in ensuring that the unemployed return to work as quickly as possible and are matched with the best possible job by providing the support to help people reenter the labor market. Through reskilling and upskilling measures, ALMPs can help direct people into areas that face skills shortages. ALMPs are a key component of "activation strategies" and typically are linked to governments' effort to smooth the school-to-work transition.[112]

Job Portals

Many European employment agencies operate job portals that match job seekers with vacancies. Several countries have moved into subcontracting, thus opening an important role for private employment agencies to resolve information failures in the labor market.[113]

Box 10: Kazakhstan—Road Map on Employment and Socialization of Youth

In 2018, the government adopted the Road Map on the Employment and Socialization of Youth not in Employment, Education, or Training (NEET), which covers citizens aged 18–29 years. Activities include (i) providing occupational orientation by establishing advisory centers for young people selecting a profession and functional reviews to guide them into promising professions; (ii) promoting technical and vocational education, improving the effectiveness of dual education, and establishing competence centers in colleges with due regard to the training of engineering personnel; (iii) raising awareness about state support and development measures, including creating a supply-and-demand map for the youth labor market and continuing the practice of holding career fairs, awareness-raising campaigns, and public consultations; (iv) developing youth entrepreneurship and introducing government grant funding of youth projects, assuming that business plans are provided; (v) encouraging military patriotic upbringing; (vi) improving the activities of youth resource centers and monitoring and expanding the NEET youth database; (vii) resolving the housing issue and creating youth housing cooperatives (including by drawing on the experience of Almaty to create regional housing programs); (viii) adapting the tools of government social order and grant financing, paying attention to supporting young single mothers to prevent child abandonment; (ix) improving methodology and legislation to consider the possibility of regulatory and legal confirmation of the NEET concept in labor legislation, conducting NEET youth-oriented studies, organizing a NEET youth register as part of the labor market's automated information system, and conducting sociological diagnostic and monitoring surveys to identify the key social dimensions of NEET youth; and (x) encouraging a healthy lifestyle (e.g., planning workout platforms in probable youth gathering areas).

Source: Official Information Source of the Prime Minister of the Republic of Kazakhstan. 2018. Government Approves Draft Roadmap for Employment and Socialization of Youth. 18 September.

---

[111] "Active labor market programs include all social expenditure (other than education) which is aimed at the improvement of the beneficiaries' prospect of finding gainful employment or to otherwise increase their earnings capacity. This category includes spending on public employment services and administration, labor market training, special programs for youth when in transition from school to work, labor market programs to provide or promote employment for unemployed and other people (excluding young and disabled people) and special programs for the disabled." OECD. 2001. *Labour Market Policies that Work*. Paris.
[112] European Commission. European Semester Thematic Factsheet: Active Labour Market Policies.
[113] Typically, public employment agencies focus on low-skilled jobs, while private agencies specialize in occupations requiring high-level qualifications and sector-specific competencies, e.g., the hospitality industry.

The development of ICT has opened new possibilities for how young people search for work and how job seekers and firms are matched. The expansion of mobile telephones has provided a basis for improving information and the intermediation of job opportunities. Technology can connect young people with jobs in other countries and offers them a chance to work in global markets without leaving their home countries.

E. Gender Equality

In formal compulsory education, female and male enrollment rates are almost equal in the five countries. However, the issue of gender inequality becomes visible at higher levels of education. In Kazakhstan, the Kyrgyz Republic, Turkmenistan, and Uzbekistan, female and male enrollment in TVET are almost equal, while in Tajikistan female participation in TVET is significantly lower than male enrollment (footnote 95). All the countries demonstrate a strong gender bias in the choice of profession or specialization made by female or male students, with female students prevailing in education, health care, and textile and garment manufacturing—all usually characterized by low salaries.

In Tajikistan, several factors contribute to the low enrollment rates of females in TVET: (i) location of facilities, (ii) lack of appropriate student accommodation, (iii) lack of courses in nontraditional subjects for which women can find work, (iv) lack of job placement support, (v) gender disparities in instructors, (vi) high costs and limited family investment in girls' education, and (vii) widespread gender stereotypes about women's employment.

In tertiary education, the gender imbalance appears to change. Kazakhstan, the Kyrgyz Republic, and Turkmenistan show a higher proportion of female students than male, while Tajikistan and Uzbekistan show a higher proportion of males than females. In employment, women in Tajikistan appear to be the most disadvantaged group. They are employed mostly in the public sector, and almost 25% are involved in unpaid work in family businesses compared with 13% of males.

Gender-responsive TVET could shift labor market segmentation by gender and reduce the gap in labor force participation by helping women acquire the skills and education necessary to transition from training into better-paying jobs.

F. Information and Communication Technology and Digital Skills

Digital skills represent a continuum of diverse skills, which can be fostered through formal education and training and through informal learning. Digital skills can be defined as the capacity to access, manage, understand, integrate, communicate, evaluate, and create information safely and appropriately.

Digital technologies have changed how organizations work, creating jobs and replacing others. Digital technologies are gradually becoming more widely used in manufacturing, construction, and energy in Central Asia. It makes a big difference for the long-term employability of the trainees, therefore, that they have a basic understanding of digital technologies such as engine fault diagnostics tools, programmable logic controls, and auto computer-aided design and computer-aided manufacturing. For workers, the change means reskilling to thrive in a high-tech working environment. For educators, the change means integrating ICT into skills development, not just in the course materials but also in course delivery. Technology can ease delivery of TVET to more people. In many countries, more than 80% of youth are online. Students can use their own digital devices to access courses through the internet.

Box 11: Increasing Gender Responsiveness of Technical and Vocational Education and Training in Viet Nam

Based on a gender assessment of the technical and vocational education and training (TVET) and school-to-work transition programs in Viet Nam, a study commissioned by ADB produced seven recommendations to guide the government, education institutions and facilities, and the private sector to support a more inclusive skilled workforce:

Change social and cultural attitudes and awareness about women working in nontraditional sectors. In addition to official initiatives to launch campaigns directed at young women and men, parents, community members, and decision makers, TVET institutions can roll out campaigns to challenge and dismantle gender-based stereotypes. The campaigns will require champions, role models, and mentors alongside social media to reach potential female trainees. The activities should align with job fairs that bring together institutions and private sector partners and with community awareness activities on the diversity of TVET programs.

Strengthen information and support for women related to education, training, and work options. The government—or other development actors—may need to explore new outreach channels to target female trainees. The outreach could include providing preenrollment and in-course counseling and supporting women in training programs, particularly in male-dominated course specializations. Labor market assessments and job placement programs can help advise women on market demands, niche skills areas, training programs, and career objectives.

Pilot strategies to recruit women into TVET programs with the explicit goal of improving their labor market outcomes. Evidence from the assessment suggests the need for more effective implementation of potential project pilots and/or expansion of existing TVET strategies, such as (i) expanding free training programs for women (including for women wanting to retrain after having children or caring for older family members), (ii) initiating and/or supporting recruitment and mentorship programs to support women entering industries dominated by men, (iii) expanding scholarship and award programs for women entering areas dominated by men, and (iv) expanding entrepreneurship training and access to finance initiatives to prepare and support women in starting their own businesses.

Actively reach out to female students from ethnic minority groups. Targeting ethnic minority groups requires a culturally sensitive approach to challenging social norms and overcoming barriers to participation in the community. The approach might best be piloted by working with teachers in primary, lower, and upper secondary schools, along with community leaders.

Implement a gender mainstreaming strategy and action plan for TVET as an integral part of the TVET strategy. The study observed the need for more systematic gender mainstreaming strategies with specific actions, targets and/or quotas, responsibilities across stakeholders and ministries, committed resource allocations, mandated sex- and age-disaggregated data collection, curriculum and resource material reforms, teacher sensitization and training, gender-responsive learning environments, and a system to prevent and respond to sexual harassment of trainees and trainers. The approach should include strengthened partnerships with industry to maximize labor market outcomes for women.

Improve collection and reporting of labor market and TVET-relevant data by sex and age group in the vocational training report. The study recommends expanding labor force surveys to better inform course development and offerings through sex- and age-disaggregated data.

Strengthen relationships with industry to promote better labor market outcomes for TVET female graduates. Responsiveness to future skills needs and projected labor market demands should be the driving force behind TVET. This requires a nimble sector with strong and diverse industry relations and partnerships to validate course curricula, teaching materials, and pedagogical approaches, and to facilitate on-the-job learning opportunities for trainees. Institutions and industry could work with women trainees to identify training approaches that respond to dual productive and reproductive roles of women, such as flexible hours and work arrangements.

Source: ADB. 2020. Enhancing Gender Responsiveness of Technical and Vocational Education and Training in Viet Nam. *ADB Brief*. 126. Manila.

Several training institutions already offer online and blended learning. Although these modes of learning are not suitable for all areas of training, they have considerable potential to increase course offerings as indicated by the fast-increasing popularity of e-learning in many countries. The advantage of utilizing digital technologies in learning is that it costs less than conventional training delivery. Digital teaching technologies such as "smart classrooms" also allow access to knowledge beyond the reach of conventional teaching methods.

The COVID-19 pandemic has clearly illustrated that TVET and skills programs do not easily migrate to distance and online learning. Despite these challenges in some contexts, the crisis provides an opportunity to develop more flexible learning solutions that make better use of distance learning and digital tools. However, the shift to online or distance learning in TVET and skills development during the pandemic is first and foremost an emergency response and not a rapid and permanent migration of programs.[114]

Box 12: Online Lifelong Education Institute, Republic of Korea

Seeking to increase the Republic of Korea's global competitiveness, the government aims to build a workforce driven by competency rather than academic qualifications. The national qualification framework maps the amount of education, training, and work experience required for each qualification in various industries. National competency standards define the levels of knowledge, skills, and attitudes expected of workers for tasks. Implementation of the standards in 2013 strengthened career-oriented vocational education in relation to academic qualifications.

The Online Lifelong Education Institute (OLEI), in the Korea University of Technology and Education, is a hub for online vocational training that specializes in technology and engineering. The institute mainly pursues interactive and experiential e-learning practices by incorporating new technologies into online learning environments. Funded by the Ministry of Employment and Labor, OLEI has developed and offered more than 200 free online courses to industrial workers and job seekers in mechanics, electronics, mechatronics, information and communication technology, design, materials, architecture, and chemistry. OLEI provides job basics courses and core courses and about 300 e-learning courses. Most of these online courses are 6-week formal vocational trainings that result in certificates; they are offered once or twice a month. Some non-certificate courses for informal learning are always available, along with a few college-credit courses. In April 2015, OLEI launched the portal website, e-koreatech. In its first year of operation, the site had more than 700,000 visitors.

OLEI focuses on teaching students how to handle industrial equipment. In the past, if a TVET institution wished to teach students how to do so, it either had to install the equipment, which is expensive, or schedule a day trip to a site that allowed students to see the equipment. In either case, learners were not able to do certain things, such as take apart and reassemble the equipment. Instructors could teach using only books, images, and video clips and could not offer many interactive hands-on activities. Recognizing the need for more hands-on learning about using industrial equipment, OLEI developed virtual training content using simulators, emulators, and virtual reality and augmented reality software. Using these ICTs, students can learn about various kinds of equipment, including macro-sized tools, ultra-mini tools, and expensive equipment that institutions cannot afford to buy, and how to stay safe in dangerous work situations. The first virtual training courses were about a type of refrigerator and the "clean-room control system." OLEI has made the virtual training content available via the online platform. OLEI has developed more than 40 virtual training courses and offers them in 141 training centers, public and private.

Source: United Nations Educational, Scientific and Cultural Organization. 2017. *Beyond Access: ICT-Enhanced Pedagogy in TVET in the Asia-Pacific*. Paris.

---

[114] P. Comyn. 2020. TVET and Skills Development in the Time of COVID-19. World Education Blog. 28 April. ILO.

Intensifying the use of ICT and teaching of digital skills is associated with considerable costs. It requires increased access by TVET institutions to equipment and software and affordable high-speed internet connection. Qualified teaching staff must be available, which is a challenge in several countries because of the low salaries of TVET teachers. The situation calls for a strategic plan for rolling out ICT and digital technologies in TVET, possibly in partnership with a development partner.

G. Strengthened Regional Cooperation

Although CAREC 2030 includes an initiative for regional collaboration on human resources, not much has happened. However, considering the legacy shared by the Central Asian countries and their close economic ties, considerable benefits are to be obtained from intensifying regional collaboration and experience sharing. In addition to TVET and higher education, labor migration is an area with obvious potential for coordination and joint initiatives.

It will probably require efforts by an international organization such as ADB to initiate the process.

References

Alshanskaya, A. 2019. Youth Labor Market in Kazakhstan: Who Is in Demand and Who Is Left on the Sidelines? *CABAR.asia*. 5 July.

Anderson, K., E. Ginting, and K. Taniguchi. 2020. *Uzbekistan—Quality Job Creation as a Cornerstone for Sustainable Economic Growth. Country Diagnostic Study.* Manila: ADB.

Asian Development Bank (ADB). 2012. *Technical Assistance Consultant's Report Project Number: 44402-01 Regional: Preparation of Sector Road Maps for Central and West Asia.* Manila.

———. 2016. *Country Partnership Strategy Tajikistan 2016–2020.* Manila.

———. 2016. Environment Assessment (Summary). *Country Partnership Strategy: Tajikistan, 2016–2020.* Manila.

———. 2017. *Proposed Grants Kyrgyz Republic: Skills for Inclusive Growth Sector Development Program.* Manila.

———. 2017. *CAREC 2030: Connecting the Region for Shared and Sustainable Development.* Manila.

———. 2017. *Country Partnership Strategy. Kazakhstan, 2017–2021. Promoting Economic Diversification, Inclusive Development, and Sustainable Growth.* Manila.

———. 2017. *Country Partnership Strategy Turkmenistan, 2017–2021. Catalyzing Regional Cooperation and Integration, and Economic Diversification.* Manila.

———. 2018. *Country Partnership Strategy: Kyrgyz Republic 2018–2022—Supporting Sustainable Growth, Inclusion, and Regional Cooperation.* Manila.

———. 2018. *State-Owned Enterprise Engagement and Reform. Thematic Evaluation.* Manila.

———. 2019. *Asian Development Outlook 2019.* Manila.

———. 2019. *Country Partnership Strategy Uzbekistan, 2019–2023. Supporting Economic Transformation Linked Document Inclusive and Sustainable Growth Assessment.* Manila.

———. 2019. *Education and Skills Development under the CAREC Program. Scoping Study.* Manila.

———. 2019. *Turkmenistan Fact Sheet.* Manila.

———. 2020. *Basic 2020 Statistics.* Manila.

———. 2020. *Uzbekistan—Country Diagnostic Study.* Manila.

References

Bhutia, S. 2020. Measuring Central Asia's Shadow economies. *Eurasianetwork*. 21 February.

CEIC. 2020. Tajikistan Education Statistics.

Dermastia, M. et al. 2017. *Value Chain Analysis of the Tourism Sector in Tajikistan*. Dushanbe.

European Training Foundation. 2006. *The Reform of Vocational Education and Training in the Republic of Tajikistan*. Torino.

————. 2010. *Migration Survey*. Torino.

————. 2016. *Continuing Professional Development for Vocational Teachers and Trainers in Turkey*. Torino.

————. 2017. *Torino Process 2016-17. Tajikistan. Executive Summary*. Torino.

————. 2017. *Tracer Studies. Evaluating the Impact of Training Programs*. Torino.

Eurasianet. 2020. Uzbekistan Pledges to Give Hopeful Migrant Laborers Loans. 19 August.

European Commission. 2017. *Overview of the Higher Education System—Kyrgyzstan*. Brussels.

————. 2017. *Overview of the Higher Education System—Turkmenistan*. Brussels.

————. 2017. *Overview of the Higher Education System—Uzbekistan*. Brussels.

European Union. No date. *European Semester Thematic Factsheet: Active Labour Market Policies*.

Fawcett, C., G. El Sawi, and C. Allison. 2014. *TVET Models, Structure and Policy Reform. Evidence from the European and Eurasia Region*. Washington, DC: USAID.

Griffin, A. and B. Bailey. 1994. Vocational Education in Russia in the Transition to a Market Economy. *The Vocational Aspect of Education*. 46 (2).

Hamby, G. R. G., D. R. Smith, E. Allworth, and D. Sinor. 2017. History of Central Asia. *Britannica*.

International Labour Organization. ILOSTAT. Labor Market Information Systems (LMIS).

International Organization for Migration (IOM). 2014. *Tajik Migrants with Re-Entry Bans to the Russian Federation*. Geneva.

————. 2018. *Current Migration Situation and Trends in Kyrgyzstan*. Geneva.

International Qualifications Assessment Service Government of Alberta. 2016. *International Education Guide*. Alberta, Canada.

Investopedia. 2020. Eurasian Economic Union.

Japan International Cooperation Agency. 2018. *Migration, Living Conditions and Skills: Panel Study Tajikistan Survey*. Dushanbe.

Organisation for Economic Co-operation and Development. 2017. *Kazakhstan: Monitoring Skills Development through Occupational Standards*. Paris.

Republic of Tajikistan. 2016. *Development Strategy up to 2030*. Dushanbe.

Sharifzoda, K. 2019. Why Is Kazakhstan a Growing Destination for Central Asian Migrant Workers? *The Diplomat*. 13 June.

SkillsFuture. https://www.skillsfuture.gov.sg/.

TajStat. 2005. *Labor Force Survey 2004*. Dushanbe

_____. 2010. *Migration Survey*. Dushanbe

_____. 2015. *Tajikistan in Figures*. Dushanbe.

_____. 2016. *The Population of the Republic of Tajikistan 2015*. Dushanbe.

_____. 2017 *Labor Force Survey 2016*. Dushanbe.

_____. 2017. *Situation in the Labour Market in the Republic of Tajikistan. Based on the results of the Labour Force Survey 2016*. Dushanbe.

_____. 2018. *Labor Market in Republic of Tajikistan*. Dushanbe.

_____. 2019. *Labor Force Survey 2018*. Dushanbe.

Team NSN. 2018. Siemens Technical Academy (STA), Mumbai – German Dual VET Transforms the Lives of Youth in India. National Skills Network. 8 October.

The Chronicle of Turkmenistan. 2019. Title of Article. 25 May.

United Nations. 2018. E-Government Development Index (accessed 10 October 2020).

United Nations Development Programme (UNDP). 2019. *Human Development Report* (accessed 12 October 2020)

_____. 2020. *Kyrgyz Republic Could See GDP Plunge 10 Percent as a Result of COVID-19, as Domestic Violence Surges*. Place of publication.

_____. 2020. *Uzbekistan's Health Care System, Economy Hit Hard by COVID-19*. Place of publication.

United Nations. Department of Economic and Social Affairs Population Dynamics (accessed 3 October 2020).

United Nations Educational, Scientific and Cultural Organization (UNESCO). 2017. *Beyond Access: ICT-Enhanced Pedagogy in TVET in the Asia-Pacific*. Paris.

UNESCO. 2020. *Ensuring Lifelong Learning for All in Kazakhstan, Kyrgyzstan, Tajikistan and Uzbekistan*. Paris.

University of Notre Dame. 2020. Global Adaptation Initiative (ND-GAIN) (accessed 8 October 2020).

University of Oxford. 2019. Oxford Poverty and Human Development Initiative. Multidimensional Poverty Index Data Bank.

UZ Daily. New Opportunities in the Education System of Uzbekistan Discussed. 4 April.

Volkov, V. 2018. Why Do the Authorities of Turkmenistan Create Obstacles for Their Migrant Workers? *Deutsche Welle*. 9 July.

World Bank. 2014. *Tajikistan: Fiscal Risks from State-Owned Enterprises. Policy Note*. Washington, DC.

_____. 2015. *Joint Country Engagement Note for Turkmenistan for the period FY16–FY17*. Washington, DC.

_____. 2018. *Growth and Job Creation in Uzbekistan – An In-Depth Diagnostic*. Washington, DC.

_____. 2018. *Kyrgyz Republic: From Vulnerability to Prosperity Systematic Country Diagnostic*. Washington, DC.

_____. 2019. *Kazakhstan Country Partnership Framework 2020–2025*. Washington, DC.

_____. 2019. *Project Information Document—Kyrgyz Republic Education Support*. Washington, DC.

_____. 2019. *Tajikistan Country Economic Memorandum: Nurturing Tajikistan's Growth Potential: Macroeconomics, Trade and Investment Global Practice Europe and Central Asia Region*. Washington, DC.

_____. 2020. *Building the Right Skills for Human Capital Education, Skills, and Productivity in the Kyrgyz Republic*. Washington, DC.

_____. 2020. *Economic Outlook Turkmenistan*. Washington, DC.

_____. 2020. *Europe and Central Asia Economic Update*. Washington, DC.

_____. 2020. *Kyrgyz Republic Economic Outlook Navigating the Crisis. Kazakhstan Economic Update*. Washington, DC.

_____. 2020. *Tajikistan Economic Overview*. Washington, DC.

_____. 2020. *Uzbekistan Economic Outlook*. Washington, DC.

_____. 2020. *World Development Indicators* (accessed 3 October 2020).

Zakharovsky, L.V. 2015. The Soviet System of Vocational Education and the Process of Mobilization Modernization in the Soviet Union. *Scientific Dialogue*. 5 (41).

www.ingramcontent.com/pod-product-compliance
Lightning Source LLC
Chambersburg PA
CBHW061139230426
43662CB00026B/2471